PENGUIN BOOKS

FIVE RINGS, SIX CRISES, SEVEN DWARFS, AND 38 WAYS TO WIN AN ARGUMENT

John Boswell is the author of nine books and the coauthor of the best-selling *What They Don't Teach You at Harvard Business School*. He lives in New York City and works in book publishing. Dan Starer, author of three books, is a professional researcher based in New York City. He has contributed research to fifty-five bestsellers in the last twelve years.

FIVE RINGS, SIX CRISES, SEVEN DWARFS, AND 38 WAYS TO WIN AN ARGUMENT:

Numerical lists you never knew or once knew
and probably forgot

BY JOHN BOSWELL
AND DANIEL STARER

PENGUIN BOOKS

PENGUIN BOOKS
Published by the Penguin Group
Viking Penguin, a division of Penguin Books USA Inc.,
375 Hudson Street, New York, New York 10014, U.S.A.
Penguin Books Ltd, 27 Wrights Lane, London W8 5TZ, England
Penguin Books Australia Ltd, Ringwood, Victoria, Australia
Penguin Books Canada Ltd, 10 Alcorn Avenue, Suite 300, Toronto, Ontario, Canada M4V 3B2
Penguin Books (N.Z.) Ltd, 182–190 Wairau Road, Auckland 10, New Zealand

Penguin Books Ltd, Registered Offices:
Harmondsworth, Middlesex, England

First published in the United States of America by
Viking Penguin, a division of Penguin Books USA Inc., 1990
Published in Penguin Books 1991

10   9   8   7   6   5   4   3   2

THE LIBRARY OF CONGRESS HAS CATALOGUED THE HARDCOVER AS FOLLOWS:
Boswell, John, 1945–
Five rings, six crises, seven dwarfs and 38 ways to win an argument: numerical listings you should know or once
knew and probably forgot/John Boswell and Dan Starer.
p. cm.
ISBN 0 14 01.3195 7(pbk.)   ISBN 0-670-83240-5(hc.)
1. Handbooks, vade-mecums, etc.   I. Starer, Dan.   II. Title.   III. Title: 5 rings, 6 crises, 7 dwarfs and 38 ways to
win an argument.   IV. Title: Numerical listings you should know or once knew and probably forgot.
AG105.B75   1990
031.02–dc20   90–50068

Printed in the United States of America
Set in Gill Sans and Walbaum
Designed by Nan Jernigan/The Colman Press

ACKNOWLEDGMENTS

Grateful acknowledgment is made for permission to use the following copyrighted material:

List of "12 Ways Wonder Bread Helps Build Strong Bodies" and illustrations used by permission of Continental Baking Co. and Ralston Purina Company.

The Pegasus, or Flying Red Horse, is a registered trademark of the Mobil Oil Corporation and is used with permission.

The Twelve Steps of Alcoholics Anonymous reprinted with permission of Alcoholic Anonymous World Services, Inc.

Excerpts from *The Five Chinese Brothers* by Claire Huchet Bishop, illustrated by Kurt Wiese. Copyright © 1938, 1963 by Coward-McCann, Inc. Reprinted by permission.

Photograph of the Four Seasons singing group reproduced with permission of Rhino Records, Inc., and Four Seasons Partnership.

Table of geological eras from *The Facts on File Dictionary of Geology and Geophysics* by Dorothy Farris Lapidus. Copyright © 1987 by Dorothy Farris Lapidus. By permission of Facts on File, Inc.

Big Eight Conference logo reproduced with permission of the Big Eight.

List of forty spaces on the MONOPOLY® game board reprinted by permission of Parker Brothers. MONOPOLY® is a registered trademark of Parker Brothers.

Logo of the 4-H Club reproduced with permission of the United States Department of Agriculture Extension Service.

Photographs of the Buddha and the San Francisco Earthquake reproduced with permission of Brown Brothers.

Photograph of the Marx brothers reproduced with permission of Culver Pictures, Inc.

Photographs of Joseph Columbo, the Chicago Eight, Secretariat, and Richard Nixon reproduced with permission of The Bettman Archive.

* * *

Special thanks to Kathryn Huse, Heather Doughty, and Robert Youdelman.

DEDICATIONS

To my wonderful wife, Maggie.

Dan Starer

To my three muses:
1. Carol
2. Jonathan
3. Gillian.

John Boswell

CONTENTS

LISTANA

It is hard to believe that there was once a time when most of us could actually name all nine types of coal. Whether from ninth-grade science or seventh-grade civics classes (remember the show-off who could name all the presidents?), memorizing lists was part of our common educational experience.

Today most of us would be hard pressed to get past *bituminous* and *anthracite*. Fortunately, in the vast majority of cases, our lives, or livelihoods, do not depend on total recall of this sort of information.

Still, there is something intrinsically fascinating about the lists we know or once knew. Perhaps it is the fact that we ever had to *care* that much about coal; more likely, it is the idea that rattling around in our brain cells somewhere are words like *lignite* and *peat*, as well as the Seventh Article of the Constitution and the symbol for Potassium.

There is also something very reassuring about numbered lists. They are so *finite*. If you can name all five Great Lakes you own that piece of knowledge. No one is ever likely to come up with Great Lake number six.

And it is comforting to know that, according to Schopenhauer, there are absolutely only thirty-eight ways to win an argument. After exhausting all thirty-eight you can admit defeat graciously, secure in the knowledge that there is no thirty-ninth stratagem.

What we have tried to do here is to collect in one place all those lists that we know or once knew—more than 250 lists in all. As a test of common knowledge it will be interesting to see how many you recognize or can recall.

Admittedly, some of the lists are not so common. Indeed, some lists such as "The Noble Eightfold Path" and "The Four Etheric Formative Forces," are downright arcane. Others, like "The Seven Warning Signs of Cancer," are merely useful. Also, in the interest of totality, many of the included lists have grown out of unique or specialized experiences such as Hebrew school, catechism class, or medical school (the one category where you hope someone still remembers all the lists).

They are almost all, however, legitimate numbered lists. We have eliminated as best we could any degree of arbitrariness—the ten best of this or the five top of that (other than, of course, The Four Tops!). The rare exceptions are such lists as "The Four Versions of 'The Three Musketeers,'" where, in the interest of space and brevity, some truncated form seemed to be in order.

The most enjoyable lists, of course, are the ones we learned outside the classroom, either to demonstrate our grasp of popular culture (the fourth Marx Brother, the fifth Beatle, the fourth, fifth, and sixth Three Stooges) or simply because they took so little effort ("The Seven Dwarfs," "Santa's Eight Reindeer"). These lists are truly a test of one's common knowledge.

One man's list may be another man's wasted brain cells, but simply contemplating the array—from "Twelve Ways Wonder Bread Builds Strong Bodies" to the "Twelve Apostles," from the "Seven Ages of Man" to the "Seven Sisters" (schools, stars, and companies)—of information, causes one to consider not only the brain's capacity for order, but its almost infinite capacity for storing the most bizarre and amazing facts. As you browse through these lists we hope you are not only amazed but amused, intrigued, challenged, entertained, and maybe even a little nostalgic.

Daniel Starer
John Boswell

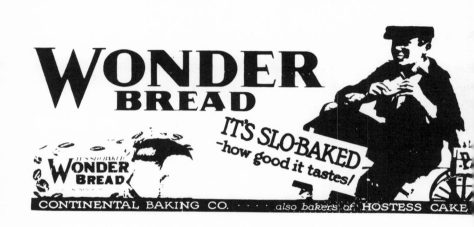

The Dynamic Duo Bruce Wayne, a playboy and philanthropist turned vigilante crime fighter, first appeared in Detective Comics #27 published by DC Comics in 1939. He later creates the Dynamic Duo when he trains Dick Grayson, a poor orphan, to become his partner. The Dynamic Duo are:

1. Batman

2. Robin

Three Men in a Tub The three men in the children's rhyme, "Three Men in a Tub," are:

1. The butcher
2. The baker

3. The candlestick maker

The Fantastic Four When we first see the Fantastic Four in Marvel Comics, four ordinary Americans are struggling to beat the Soviets into space. When their spacecraft passes through cosmic rays, these four characters find they have superpowers. Two animated TV series grew out of this comic book. The original members were:

1. Mr. Fantastic
2. Invisible Girl

3. The Human Torch
4. The Thing

Seven Soldiers of Victory

These DC Comics heroes have made appearances since 1941, and are most often seen fighting the Axis Powers in World War II. The Seven are:

1. Crimson Avenger
2. Green Arrow
3. Speedy
4. Shining Knight
5. Star-Spangled Kid
6. Stripesy
7. Vigilante

Santa's Eight Reindeer

In Clement Moore's poem "A Visit from St. Nicholas," Santa calls out the names of his eight reindeer. The names of these reindeer are:

1. Blitzen
2. Comet
3. Cupid
4. Dancer
5. Dasher
6. Donder
7. Prancer
8. Vixen

A ninth reindeer, Rudolph, is sometimes added in inclement weather, from the song "Rudolph the Red-Nosed Reindeer."

Ten Little Indians

In a subtracting counting rhyme, the Ten Little Indians meet various fates which take them out of the count:

10. One goes home (leaving nine, etc.)
9. One falls off a gate

8. One goes to sleep
7. One breaks his neck
6. One kicks the bucket
5. One falls into the cellar
4. One gets fuddled
3. One falls out of a canoe
2. One gets shot by the first
1. One gets married, "and then there were none"

Ten little Indians, from a nineteenth-century drawing

The Ten National Holidays   In the United States these ten days are officially designated national holidays:

1. New Year's Day, January 1
2. Martin Luther King, Jr.'s Birthday, January 15 *

3. Washington's Birthday, February 22 *
4. Memorial Day, May 30
5. Independence Day, July 4
6. Labor Day, the first Monday in September
7. Columbus Day, October 12 *
8. Veterans Day, November 11
9. Thanksgiving Day, the fourth Thursday in November
10. Christmas Day, December 25

*This day is observed on the Monday closest to the date given.

The Twelve Birthstones

Month	*Birthstone*
1. January	Garnet
2. February	Amethyst
3. March	Aquamarine or bloodstone
4. April	Diamond
5. May	Emerald
6. June	Pearl, moonstone, or alexandrite
7. July	Ruby
8. August	Sardonyz or peridot
9. September	Sapphire
10. October	Opal or tourmaline
11. November	Topaz
12. December	Turquoise or lapis lazuli

The Twelve Days of Christmas

On each of the twelve days of Christmas (from Christmas Day to the Epiphany), the "true love" in this popular Christmas song sends a new gift along with the ones already sent, so that by the twelfth day, the whole list is repeated. In order from the first day, the gifts are:

1. A partridge in a pear tree
2. Two turtle doves
3. Three French hens
4. Four calling birds
5. Five golden rings
6. Six geese a-laying
7. Seven swans a-swimming
8. Eight maids a-milking
9. Nine drummers drumming
10. Ten pipers piping
11. Eleven ladies dancing
12. Twelve lords a-leaping

The Twelve Ways Wonder Bread™ Helps Build Strong Bodies

In the 1950s and 1960s Wonder Bread™, a famous brand of white bread, used an advertising campaign that claimed one serving had 12 nutritional values. Their list, popular at the time though dated by today's standards, claimed Wonder Bread builds strong bodies in these ways:

1. Muscle—as much Protein as a serving of roast sirloin of beef.
2. Bones & Teeth—as much Calcium for bones and teeth as in a helping of cottage cheese.

3. Body Cells—as much Phosphorus for cell metabolism as in one egg.

4. Blood—as much Iron for rich, red blood as found in three lamb chops.

5. Appetite—as much Vitamin B1 to help maintain appetite as supplied by a serving of fried liver.

6. Growth—as much Vitamin B2 for growth processes as provided by three slices of yellow American cheese.

7. Brain—as much Niacin to help maintain mental health as found in six sardines.

8. Energy—as much Energy as supplied by the carbohydrates, fat and protein in two glasses of milk.

9. Red Cells—as much Copper for hemoglobin generation as in one banana.

10. Vitamin B12—as much Cobalt for B12 synthesis as in one serving of green peas.

11. Protein (Digestion)—as much Manganese to aid enzyme activity for protein digestion as in a liberal serving of lettuce.

12. Tissue (Respiration)—as much Zinc for enzyme formation to aid tissue respiration as in two and one-half tablespoonfuls of peanut butter.

Helps build strong bodies 12 ways®

The Twenty-five Wedding Anniversary Gifts

Although there is no official list, many experts on etiquette agree that it is proper to give these gifts on the following wedding anniversaries:

Anniversary	Gift
1st	Paper
2nd	Cotton or calico
3rd	Leather
4th	Linen or silk
5th	Wood
6th	Iron
7th	Copper, brass, or wool
8th	Bronze
9th	Pottery
10th	Tin
11th	Steel
12th	Silk or linen
13th	Lace
14th	Ivory
15th	Crystal or glass
20th	China
25th	Silver
30th	Pearls
35th	Coral or jade
40th	Rubies or garnets
45th	Sapphires or tourmalines
50th	Gold

Anniversary	*Gift*
55th	Emeralds or turquoise
60th	Diamonds or gold
75th	Diamonds or gold

AMERICAN HISTORY

The Big Three

In 1919 representatives from France, Great Britain, and the United States met at the Paris Peace Conference to negotiate the Treaty of Versailles. The representatives of these countries were called The Big Three:

1. Premier Georges Clemenceau
2. Prime Minister David Lloyd George
3. President Woodrow Wilson

During World War II the leaders of Great Britain, the United States, and the Soviet Union were *also* named The Big Three:

1. Prime Minister Winston Churchill
2. President Franklin D. Roosevelt
3. Premier Josef Stalin

———

The Three Branches of Government

The Constitution of the United States historically divides the federal government into these branches:

1. Legislative
2. Executive

3. Judicial

The Big Four

After World War II these four countries were designated The Big Four because of their importance:

1. Great Britain
2. France
3. Soviet Union
4. United States

The Four Freedoms

In his State of the Union address to Congress on January 6, 1941, President Franklin D. Roosevelt set forth four basic freedoms for the American public. They were:

1. freedom of speech and expression
2. freedom of the individual to worship God in his own way
3. freedom from want
4. freedom from fear

The Big-Five Packers

The Big-Five Packers were five companies that, in 1919, were found to have controlled the butter and eggs, oleomargarine, cottonseed oil, fertilizer, perfume, and leather novelties industries. In 1920 the Supreme Court enjoined them from any other business besides their original meat-packing operations. The Big-Five Packers were:

1. Armour
2. Cudahy
3. Morris
4. Swift
5. Wilson

The Five Civilized Nations

Five Indian nations were resettled from their homelands to the Indian territory (now Oklahoma) from 1830 to 1840. These nations were:

1. the Cherokee
2. the Chickasaw
3. the Choctaw
4. the Creek
5. the Seminole

Nixon's Six Crises

Richard Nixon's best-selling book, published in 1962, was divided into six chapters, each describing a major challenge in his life. The chapter headings in *Six Crises* are:

1. "The Hiss Case," in which Congressman Nixon gained public notice by pursuing Whittaker Chambers's spying accusations against Alger Hiss.
2. "The Fund," in which bad publicity regarding a secret slush fund that Nixon controlled in 1952 nearly made him withdraw as the Republican nominee for Vice-President.
3. "The Heart Attack," in which Nixon became a caretaker president as Eisenhower recovered from a heart attack in September, 1952.
4. "Caracas," in which Pat and Richard Nixon were attacked during a visit to the capital of Venezuela.

5. "Khrushchev," in which Nixon confronted the Soviet leader in the famed "kitchen debate."
6. "The Campaign of 1960," in which Nixon lost the presidential election to John F. Kennedy by a tiny margin.

Nixon's sixth crisis: during the 1960 presidential debate

The Seven Articles of the United States Constitution

Article 1.

Section 1 states legislative powers are vested in Congress.

Section 2 describes how members of the House of Representatives are chosen, the number and qualifications of representatives, how taxes are apportioned, how vacancies are to be filled, who chooses officers in the House, and who has the power to impeach.

Section 3 describes how senators are chosen, their qualifications, officers of the Senate, and the impeachment and trial of the president.

Section 4 describes the times and manner of holding elections in Congress.

Section 5 covers membership, quorum, adjournments, and rules.

Section 6 covers compensation, privileges, and situations for disqualification of members of Congress.

Section 7 describes the procedures for passing bills in Congress.

Section 8 describes the powers of Congress.

Section 9 covers immigration, habeas corpus (illegal imprisonment), apportionment of taxes; and prohibits bills of attainder (which restrict civil liberties for those convicted of murder or treason), export duties between states, the government from granting titles of nobility, and officials from accepting gifts from foreign governments.

Section 10 prohibits the states from certain powers and acts.

Article 2.

Section 1 describes the president's term of office, procedure for election, qualifications, next-in-power, compensation, and oath of office.

Section 2 describes the president's power as commander-in-chief, use of cabinet officers, treaty-making power, nomination of officers, and power to fill Senate vacancies.

Section 3 describes the president's power to convene and adjourn Congress, receive ambassadors, execute laws, and commission officers.

Section 4 states the president and all civil officers must be removed from office for certain crimes if convicted and impeached.

Article 3.

Section 1 covers the tenure and compensation of judges.

Section 2 describes the extent of judicial power, jurisdiction of the Supreme Court, appellate jurisdiction, and trial by jury.

Section 3 defines treason and punishment for it.

Article 4.

Section 1 requires each state to respect the acts and judicial proceedings of other states.

Section 2 describes the privileges of citizens in a state and the requirement that fugitives be delivered up between states.

Section 3 describes admission of new states, and the power of Congress over territory and property.

Section 4 guarantees each state the republican form of government.

Article 5.

Describes how the Constitution can be revised.

Article 6.

Declares prior debts valid; the Constitution and laws of the United States to be supreme; requires members of Congress to take an oath in support of the Constitution; prohibits a religious test as qualification for public office.

Article 7.

Describes the ratification needed to establish the Constitution.

Twelve Gray-Haired Guys Named George

When President Nixon's cabinet was announced in December 1968, *Time* magazine named them "twelve gray-haired guys named George" because the men were so uniformly bland. The twelve were:

1. Winton M. Blount (Postmaster General)
2. Robert H. Finch (Health, Education and Welfare)
3. Clifford M. Hardin (Agriculture)
4. Walter J. Hickel (Interior)
5. David M. Kennedy (Treasury)
6. Melvin R. Laird (Defense)
7. John N. Mitchell (Attorney General)
8. William P. Rogers (State)
9. George Romney (Housing)

10. George P. Schultz (Labor)
11. Maurice H. Stans (Commerce)
12. John A. Volpe (Transportation)

The Thirteen Original Colonies

The British Colonies established before the start of the American Revolutionary War are known as the Thirteen Original Colonies. They are represented in the flag of the United States by the thirteen stripes—six white and seven red. The Colonies were:

1. Connecticut
2. Delaware
3. Georgia
4. Maryland
5. Massachusetts
6. New Hampshire
7. New Jersey
8. New York
9. North Carolina
10. Pennsylvania
11. Rhode Island
12. South Carolina
13. Virginia

Wilson's Fourteen Points

At the end of World War I, President Woodrow Wilson gave a speech before both houses of Congress that outlined his program for peace. His Fourteen Points were:

1. "Open covenants openly arrived at"
2. Freedom of the seas
3. Removal of economic barriers between all nations of the world

4. Arms reduction
5. A consideration of colonial claims to account for the wishes of local inhabitants and their rivals
6. Evacuation and restoration of conquered territories in Russia
7. Maintaining the sovereignty of Belgium
8. Settlement of the Alsace-Lorraine question
9. Redrawing the frontiers of Italy with consideration for local nationalities
10. Dividing Austria-Hungary with consideration for its nationalities
11. Redrawing the boundaries of the Balkan states
12. Limiting Turkey's control over its own people and ensuring freedom to navigate the Dardanelles
13. Establishing an independent Poland with free access to the ocean
14. Establishing "a general association of nations"

The League of Nations came about as a result of this last point.

The Twenty-six Amendments to the Constitution

The ten original amendments constitute the Bill of Rights.

Amendment 1. Prohibits Congress from passing laws that restrict religious freedoms. Guarantees freedom of speech, of the press, and the right to petition.

Amendment 2.   Guarantees the right to keep and bear arms.

Amendment 3.   Restricts soldiers from being quartered in private homes without the owner's consent.

Amendment 4.   Guarantees against unreasonable search and seizure.

Amendment 5.   Prohibits criminal prosecution without a Grand Jury hearing and the taking of private property without just compensation.

Amendment 6.   Guarantees the right to a speedy trial, a jury of one's peers, to be confronted with witnesses, and to have defense counsel.

Amendment 7.   Guarantees the right to a jury trial in civil matters worth more than $20.

Amendment 8.   Prohibits excessive bail, fines, or cruel and unusual punishment.

Amendment 9.   States the rights enumerated in the Constitution shall not deny the rights of others.

Amendment 10.   States all other rights belong to the states, or the people.

Amendment 11. Limits judicial power.

Amendment 12. Describes how president and vice-president are chosen.

Amendment 13. Abolishes slavery.

Amendment 14. Protects against the abridgment of citizenship rights.

Amendment 15. States that race is no bar to voting rights.

Amendment 16. Authorizes income taxes.

Amendment 17. States that senators are to be elected by direct popular vote.

Amendment 18. Prohibits the manufacture and sale of liquor.

Amendment 19. Gives the vote to women in national elections.

Amendment 20. States the terms in office of president, vice-president, and senators.

Amendment 21. Repeals the Eighteenth Amendment.

Amendment 22. Limits the president to two terms in office.

Amendment 23.   Grants the right to vote in presidential elections to the District of Columbia.

Amendment 24.   Guarantees the right to vote in federal elections despite a citizen's failure to pay taxes.

Amendment 25.   States the procedure and order of succession if a president is disabled.

Amendment 26.   Lowers the voting age to eighteen.

The Forty-one Presidents

Presidents	Dates of Service
1. George Washington	Apr. 30, 1789–Mar. 3, 1797
2. John Adams	Mar. 4, 1797–Mar. 3, 1801
3. Thomas Jefferson	Mar. 4, 1801–Mar. 3, 1805
	Mar. 4, 1805–Mar. 3, 1809

Presidents	*Dates of Service*
4. James Madison	Mar. 4, 1809–Mar. 3, 1813
	Mar. 4, 1813–Mar. 3, 1817
5. James Monroe	Mar. 4, 1817–Mar. 3, 1825
6. John Quincy Adams	Mar. 4, 1825–Mar. 3, 1829
7. Andrew Jackson	Mar. 4, 1829–Mar. 3, 1833
	Mar. 4, 1833–Mar. 3, 1837
8. Martin Van Buren	Mar. 4, 1837–Mar. 3, 1841
9. William Henry Harrison	Mar. 4, 1841–Apr. 4, 1841
10. John Tyler	Apr. 6, 1841–Mar. 3, 1845
11. James K. Polk	Mar. 4, 1845–Mar. 3, 1849
12. Zachary Taylor	Mar. 5, 1849–July 9, 1850
13. Millard Fillmore	July 10, 1850–Mar. 3, 1853
14. Franklin Pierce	Mar. 4, 1853–Mar. 3, 1857
15. James Buchanan	Mar. 4, 1857–Mar. 3, 1861
16. Abraham Lincoln	Mar. 4, 1861–Mar. 3, 1865
	Mar. 4, 1865–Apr, 15, 1865

PRESIDENT OF THE UNITED STATES

ABRAHAM LINCOLN

Presidents	Dates of Service
17. Andrew Johnson	Apr. 15, 1865–Mar. 3, 1869
18. Ulysses S. Grant	Mar. 4, 1869–Mar. 3, 1873
	Mar. 4, 1873–Mar. 3, 1877
19. Rutherford B. Hayes	Mar. 4, 1877–Mar. 3, 1881
20. James A. Garfield	Mar. 4, 1881–Sept. 19, 1881
21. Chester A. Arthur	Sept. 20, 1881–Mar. 3, 1885
22. Grover Cleveland	Mar. 4, 1885–Mar. 3, 1889
23. Benjamin Harrison	Mar. 4, 1889–Mar. 3, 1893
24. Grover Cleveland	Mar. 4, 1893–Mar. 3, 1897
25. William McKinley	Mar. 4, 1897–Mar. 3, 1901
	Mar. 4, 1901–Sept. 14, 1901
26. Theodore Roosevelt	Sept. 14, 1901–Mar. 3, 1905
	Mar. 4, 1905–Mar. 3, 1909
27. William H. Taft	Mar. 4, 1909–Mar. 3, 1913
28. Woodrow Wilson	Mar. 4, 1913–Mar. 3, 1917
	Mar. 14, 1917–Mar. 3, 1921
29. Warren G. Harding	Mar. 4, 1921–Aug. 2, 1923
30. Calvin Coolidge	Aug. 3, 1923–Mar. 3, 1925
	Mar. 4, 1925–Mar. 3, 1929
31. Herbert C. Hoover	Mar. 4, 1929–Mar. 3, 1933
32. Franklin D. Roosevelt	Mar. 4, 1933–Jan. 20, 1941
	Jan. 20, 1941–Jan. 20, 1945
	Jan. 20, 1945–Apr. 12, 1945
33. Harry S Truman	Apr. 12, 1945–Jan. 20, 1949
	Jan. 20, 1949–Jan. 20, 1953
34. Dwight D. Eisenhower	Jan. 20, 1953–Jan. 20, 1961
35. John F. Kennedy	Jan. 20, 1961–Nov. 22, 1963

36.	Lyndon B. Johnson	Nov. 22, 1963–Jan. 20, 1965
37.	Richard M. Nixon	Jan. 20, 1965–Jan. 20, 1969
		Jan. 20, 1969–Jan. 20, 1973
38.	Gerald R. Ford	Jan. 20, 1973–Aug. 9, 1974
39.	Jimmy Carter	Aug. 9, 1974–Jan. 20, 1977
40.	Ronald Reagan	Jan. 20, 1977–Jan. 20, 1981
		Jan. 20, 1981–Jan. 20, 1985
		Jan. 20, 1985–Jan. 20, 1989
41.	George Bush	Jan. 20, 1989–

The Forty-four Vice-Presidents

Vice-Presidents	*Inaugurations*
1. John Adams	1789
2. Thomas Jefferson	1797
3. Aaron Burr	1801
4. George Clinton	1805
5. Elbridge Gerry	1813
6. Daniel D. Thompkins	1817
7. John C. Calhoun	1825
8. Martin Van Buren	1833
9. Richard M. Johnson	1837
10. John Tyler	1841

Vice-Presidents	*Inaugurations*
11. George M. Dallas	1845
12. Millard Fillmore	1849
13. William R. King	1853
14. John C. Breckinridge	1857
15. Hannibal Hamlin	1861
16. Andrew Johnson	1865
17. Schuyler Colfax	1869
18. Henry Wilson	1873
19. William A. Wheeler	1877
20. Chester A. Arthur	1881
21. Thomas A. Hendricks	1885
22. Levi P. Morton	1889
23. Adlai E. Stevenson	1893
24. Garret A. Hobart	1897
25. Theodore Roosevelt	1901
26. Charles W. Fairbanks	1905
27. James S. Sherman	1909
28. Thomas R. Marshall	1913
29. Calvin Coolidge	1921
30. Charles G. Dawes	1925
31. Charles Curtis	1929
32. John Nance Garner	1933
33. Henry Agard Wallace	1941
34. Harry S. Truman	1945
35. Alben W. Barkley	1949
36. Richard M. Nixon	1953
37. Lyndon B. Johnson	1961

Vice-Presidents	*Inaugurations*
38. Hubert H. Humphrey	1965
39. Spiro T. Agnew	1969
40. Gerald R. Ford	1973
41. Nelson A. Rockefeller	1974
42. Walter F. Mondale	1977
43. George Bush	1981
44. Dan Quayle	1989

ASTRONOMY

The *Seven Sisters*, from a German manuscript of the 1400s

The Four Classes of Galaxies

The American astronomer Edwin P. Hubble first proposed this system in 1925. The four classes are:

1. Elliptical galaxies, which appear as an elliptical disk with no spiral arms. They are the most abundant type of galaxy.
2. Spiral galaxies, which have a nucleus with arms spiraling outward. Our own Milky Way is of this type.
3. Barred Spiral galaxies, an unusual type of spiral in which a bright bar appears to slice across the nucleus.
4. Irregular galaxies, which include various rare types that do not fit into the first three classes.

The Seven Stars of the Big Dipper

Composing perhaps the most famous figure in the night sky, these seven bright stars of the Ursa Major constellation are known as Septentriones, the Wagon, Plow, or the Big Dipper. The Seven Stars of the Big Dipper, from the tip of the handle to the end of the cup, are named:

1. Benetnash
2. Mizar and Alcor (a double star)
3. Alioth
4. Megrez
5. Phecda
6. Merak
7. Dubhe

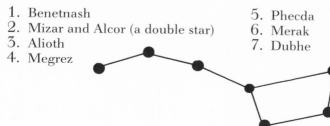

The Seven Sisters   Also called the Pleiades, these bright stars in the Taurus constellation are named:

1. Alcyone
2. Maia
3. Atlas
4. Electra

5. Merope
6. Pleione
7. Taygete

———

The Nine Planets in Our Solar System   Ranging from nearest to farthest from the sun, the planets are:

1. *Mercury*—36 million miles from the sun, orbits the sun every 88 days, 3,100 miles in diameter.
2. *Venus*—67 million miles from the sun, orbits the sun every 255 days, 7,700 miles in diameter
3. *Earth*—93 million miles from the sun, orbits the sun every 365 days, 7,920 miles in diameter
4. *Mars*—141 million miles from the sun, orbits the sun every 687 days, 4,200 miles in diameter
5. *Jupiter*—483 million miles from the sun, orbits the sun every 11.9 years, 88,640 miles in diameter
6. *Saturn*—886 million miles from the sun, orbits the sun every 29.5 years, 74,500 miles in diameter
7. *Uranus*—1,782 million miles from the sun, orbits the sun every 84 years, 32,000 miles in diameter

8. *Neptune*—2,793 million miles from the sun, orbits the sun
   every 165 days, 31,000 miles in diameter
9. *Pluto*—3,670 million miles from the sun, orbits the sun every
   248 years, 1,500 miles in diameter.

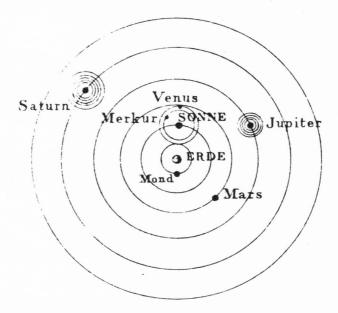

The planets (plus the sun and the moon) pre-Copernicus, when the earth was the center of
the universe

**The
Seventeen Apollo
Missions**

This United States space program to visit the moon was first proposed to Congress by President Kennedy in 1961. The first six Apollo flights were unmanned missions to test the Saturn launch rockets, the command module, and the lunar-landing module. The manned missions were:

Apollo 7. Astronauts Schirra, Eisele, and Cunningham test command and service module in earth orbit, October 1968.

Apollo 8. Astronauts Borman, Lovell, and Anders are first humans in lunar orbit, December 1968.

Apollo 9. Astronauts McDivitt, Scott, and Schweickart test lunar module in earth orbit, March 1969.

Apollo 10. Astronauts Stafford, Young, and Cernan test lunar module in lunar orbit, May 1969.

Apollo 11. Astronauts Armstrong and Aldrin are first humans to land on moon, at Mount Tranquillitatis, on July 20, 1969. Astronaut Collins remains in lunar orbit.

Apollo 12. Astronauts Conrad and Bean land at Ocean Procellarum, on November 19, 1969. They collect pieces of earlier probe, Surveyor 3. Astronaut Gordon remains in lunar orbit.

Apollo 13. Astronauts Lovell, Swigert, and Haise abort mission in April 1970, after an explosion aboard service module.

Apollo 14. Astronauts Shepard and Mitchell land at the Fra Maura formation, January 31, 1971. They collect 25 million-year-old rocks from the Cone crater. Astronaut Roosa remains in lunar orbit.

Apollo 15. Astronauts Scott and Irwin land at Hadley Rille, July 30, 1971. They drill for rock beneath the surface and use the Lunar Roving Vehicle for the first time. Astronaut Worden remains in lunar orbit.

Apollo 16. Astronauts Young and Duke land at Cayley-Descartes, April 21, 1972, the first visit to the lunar highlands. Astronaut Mattingly remains in lunar orbit.

Apollo 17. Astronauts Cernan and Schmitt land at Taurus-Littrow, December 11, 1972. Schmitt is first scientist to visit the moon. Astronaut Evans remains in orbit.

———

The Eighty-eight Constellations

Constellation	*English Name*
1. Andromeda	Andromeda (Chained Lady)
2. Antlia	Air Pump
3. Apus	Bird of Paradise
4. Aquarius	Water Bearer
5. Aquila	Eagle
6. Ara	Altar
7. Aries	Ram
8. Auriga	Charioteer
9. Bootes	Herdsman
10. Caelum	Chisel
11. Camelopardalis	Giraffe
12. Cancer	Crab
13. Canis Venatici	Hunting Dogs
14. Canis Major	Large Dog
15. Canis Minor	Small Dog

Constellation	*English Name*
16. Capricornus	Goat
17. Carina	Keel
18. Cassiopeia	Cassiopeia (Seated Lady)

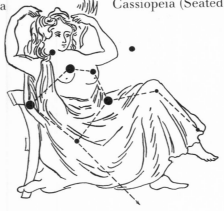

19. Centaurus	Centaur
20. Cepheus	Cepheus (the King)
21. Cetus	Whale
22. Chameleon	Chameleon
23. Circinus	Pair of Compasses
24. Columba	Dove
25. Coma Berenices	Berenice's Hair
26. Corona Australis	Southern Crown
27. Corona Borealis	Northern Crown
28. Corvus	Crow
29. Crater	Cup
30. Crux	Southern Cross

Constellation   *English Name*

	Constellation	English Name
31.	Cygnus	Swan
32.	Delphinus	Dolphin
33.	Dorado	Dorado (Swordfish)
34.	Draco	Dragon
35.	Equuleus	Colt
36.	Eridanus	Eridanus (River)
37.	Fornax	Furnace
38.	Gemini	Twins
39.	Grus	Crane
40.	Hercules	Hercules
41.	Horologium	Clock
42.	Hydra	Water Monster
43.	Hydrus	Water Snake
44.	Indus	Indian
45.	Lacerta	Lizard
46.	Leo	Lion
47.	Leo Minor	Small Lion
48.	Lepus	Hare
49.	Libra	Balance
50.	Lupus	Wolf
51.	Lynx	Lynx
52.	Lyra	Lyre
53.	Mensa	Table
54.	Microscopium	Microscope
55.	Monoceros	Unicorn
56.	Musca	Fly
57.	Norma	T-square
58.	Octans	Octant
59.	Ophiuchus	Serpent Holder

Constellation	*English Name*
60. Orion	Orion (the Hunter)
61. Pavo	Peacock
62. Pegasus	Pegasus (Winged Horse)
63. Perseus	Perseus (Rescuer of Andromeda)
64. Phoenix	Phoenix
65. Pictor	Painter's Easel
66. Pisces	Fishes
67. Piscis Austinus	Southern Fish
68. Puppis	Stern
69. Pyxis	Mariner's Compass
70. Reticulum	Net
71. Sagitta	Arrow
72. Sagittarius	Archer
73. Scorpius	Scorpion
74. Sculptor	Sculptor's Workshop
75. Scutum	Shield
76. Serpens	Serpent
77. Sextans	Sextant
78. Taurus	Bull
79. Telescopium	Telescope
80. Triangulum	Triangle
81. Triangulum Australe	Southern Triangle
82. Tucana	Toucan
83. Ursa Major	Large Bear
84. Ursa Minor	Small Bear
85. Vela	Sails
86. Virgo	Virgin
87. Volans	Flying Fish
88. Vulpecula	Little Fox

BUSINESS, JOURNALISM, AND LAW

Alfred B. Nobel, 1833–1896

The Five W's

The Five W's, standing for those questions that should be answered in any news article, are:

1. Who
2. What
3. Where
4. When
5. Why

Five Freedoms of the Air

Agreements between most countries concerning air transportation are based on five accepted rights that are called the Five Freedoms of the Air. They are:

1. The right to fly through the air space of a foreign country without landing.
2. The right to land in a foreign country for refueling and repair.
3. The freedom to discharge cargo, mail, and passengers in a foreign country.
4. The freedom to pick up cargo, mail, and passengers in a foreign country.
5. The freedom to transport cargo, mail, and passengers from one foreign country to another.

The Six Categories of Nobel Prizes

Originally, this prize was awarded in only five categories. In 1969 the sixth was added. The six categories are:

1. Peace
2. Chemistry
3. Physics
4. Physiology or Medicine
5. Literature
6. Economics

The Seven Sisters

The Seven Sisters is a collective nickname given to the seven largest oil companies. These companies are, in alphabetical order:

1. British Petroleum
2. Gulf Oil
3. Mobil Oil
4. Shell Oil
5. Standard Oil of California
6. Standard Oil of New Jersey
7. Texaco

Since the nickname was first used, Gulf Oil has been broken up, part of it being purchased by Cumberland Farms.

The Big Eight

In American business, The Big Eight has been the code word for the eight largest CPA accounting firms. These eight firms were:

1. Arthur Andersen & Co.
2. Arthur Young & Co.
3. Coopers & Lybrand
4. Deloitte, Haskins & Sells
5. Ernst & Whinney
6. Peat, Marwick, Mitchell & Co.
7. Price, Waterhouse
8. Touche, Ross & Co.

Several of these firms have merged in recent years.

The Gang of Nine

In 1988 nine companies formed a consortium to combat IBM's dominance in the microcomputer industry. This Gang of Nine created a new data pathway, or "bus" technology, called Extended Industry Standard Architecture to challenge IBM's version known as Micro Channel Architecture. The nine companies are:

1. AST Research
2. Compaq Computer Corp.
3. Epson America
4. Hewlett-Packard
5. NEC Information Technology
6. Olivetti and Co.
7. Tandy Corp.
8. Wyse Technology
9. Zenith Data Systems

Nine Points of the Law

"Possession is nine points of the law" or, in other words, possession is as good as:

1. a good cause
2. the money necessary to pursue and win a claim
3. the patience to carry a suit through the court
4. a good lawyer
5. a good counsel
6. good witnesses
7. a good jury
8. a good judge
9. good luck!

The alternative expression is "Possession is nine-tenths of the law," implying that a claimant would have to pursue the nine points to regain the tenth, ownership.

The Fourteen Categories of Pulitzer Prizes

These prizes have been awarded annually since 1917, when the estate of Joseph Pulitzer provided the funds. Administered by the Columbia University Graduate School of Journalism, eight prizes are given in journalism for work published in United States newspapers, five in literature for books with American themes, and one in music. The fourteen categories are:

1. Distinguished service by an American newspaper
2. Local reporting written under a deadline

3. Local reporting not written under a deadline
4. Reporting on national affairs
5. Reporting on international affairs
6. Editorial writing
7. Cartooning
8. News photography
9. A novel by an American
10. A play by an American
11. A book about United States history
12. A biography or autobiography
13. A volume of verse
14. A work of music

The *Four Riders of the Apocalypse*, by Albrecht Dürer

The Three Magi   Also known as the Three Wise Men, the three Magi are the eastern kings who followed the Star of Bethlehem to find the King of the Jews, and who found the baby Jesus. Their names are:

1. Gaspar, "the white one"
2. Melchior, "king of light"
3. Balthazar, "king of treasures"

The gifts they brought were frankincense, gold, and myrrh.

———

The Trinity   The Trinity is, in the Christian faith, the union of the three divine persons, or figures, in one Godhead. They are:

1. The Father
2. The Son
3. The Holy Ghost

———

The Four Evangelists   The Four Evangelists are:

1. Matthew
2. Mark
3. Luke
4. John

They are often symbolized respectively by a man, a lion, an ox, and an eagle (Revelations 4:6–10).

The Four Horsemen of the Apocalypse

According to the Revelation of St. John the Divine, the Four Horsemen of the Apocalypse are:

1. Pestilence, who rides a white horse and carries a bow and a crown.
2. War, who rides a red horse and wields the great sword.
3. Famine, who is astride a black horse and carries balancing or weighing scales.
4. Death, who rides a pale horse, and carries Hell with him.

(Revelation 6)

The Six Apostolic Fathers

The Six Apostolic Fathers were early leaders of the Christian Church. They were taught directly either by the Apostles or by their disciples. The Fathers were:

1. Barnabas
2. Clement of Rome
3. Hermas
4. Ignatius
5. Papias
6. Polycarp

The Six Days of Creation

As described in Genesis, God took six days to create the earth:

1. On the first day, He created light and dark, Day and Night.
2. On the second day, He made the firmament, dividing the waters, the firmament He called Heaven.
3. On the third day, He made the Earth, and the Seas, and grasses, herbs, and trees upon the earth.
4. On the fourth day, He made the Stars and the Sun and the Moon.
5. On the fifth day, God created the creatures of the sea and the air, the fish and the fowl.
6. On the sixth day, God created the beasts of the earth and He created man.

On the seventh day, He rested. (Genesis 1:1–31; 2:1–3)

The Seven Canonical Hours

In accordance with the Scriptures, there are seven hours or offices of specialized prayer designated by canonical law: "Seven times a day do I praise thee, because of thy righteous judgments" (Psalms 119:164). These seven hours are:

1. Matins and lauds
2. Prime
3. Tierce
4. Sext
5. Nones
6. Vespers
7. Compline

In the Anglican church, according to the Book of Common Prayer, the first two offices—matins and lauds and prime—have been combined into the Morning Prayer and the last two—vespers and compline—form the Evening Prayer.

Christ's Seven Last Sayings on the Cross

According to the Gospels of the New Testament, Jesus spoke seven times on the Cross:

1. "Father, forgive them: for they know not what they do" (Luke 23:34).
2. "Today, thou shalt be with me in paradise" (Luke 23:43).
3. "Woman, behold thy son!" (John 19:26).
4. "My God, my God why hast thou forsaken me?" (Matthew 27:46; Mark 15:34).

5. "I thirst" (John 19:28).
6. "It is finished" (John 19:30).
7. "Father into Thy Hands I commend my spirit" (Luke 23:46).

The Seven Deadly Sins

Also known as the cardinal sins, the seven deadly sins are serious moral offenses that can cause the death of the soul. They are:

1. Pride
2. Lust
3. Gluttony
4. Anger
5. Envy
6. Sloth
7. Covetousness

Deadly sin number seven (Covetousness)

The Seven Joys of Mary

In canonical tradition, Mary had seven joys:

1. The Annunciation, when the Angel Gabriel announced that she would be with child (Luke 1:26–38)
2. The Visitation, the visit of the Virgin Mary to her cousin Elizabeth, who was also with child (Luke 1:39–56)
3. The Nativity, or the birth of Christ
4. The Adoration of the Magi, when the Three Wise Men arrived bearing gifts for the King of the Jews (Matthew 2:11)
5. The Presentation in the Temple (Luke 2:25–39)
6. The Finding of the Lost Child Jesus in the temple where he had been astonishing the elders with his learning (Luke 2:42–51)
7. The Assumption, when the Virgin Mary arose bodily into Heaven

———

The Seven Sorrows of Mary

Along with her seven joys, Mary faced seven sorrows:

1. The Prophecy at the Temple, made by Simeon (Luke 2:25–39)
2. The Flight into Egypt to escape Herod's slaughter of the children of Bethlehem (Matthew 2:13–21)
3. Jesus Lost in the Temple, when he was missing from his parents for three days (Luke 2:25–93)

4. The Betrayal by Judas Iscariot (Luke 22:1–53)
5. The Crucifixion
6. The Taking Down from the Cross (Mark 15:42–47)
7. The Ascension, when Christ ascended into Heaven (Luke 24:50–53)

The Seven Holy Sacraments

Historically, in the Christian church, the Holy Sacraments are seven rites or acts that lead to grace, having been either observed or performed by Jesus in His life. They are:

1. Baptism
2. Confirmation
3. Communion (or the Eucharist)
4. Penance
5. Holy Orders
6. Matrimony
7. Extreme Unction (Last Rites)

The Seven Virtues

These acts or qualities of moral excellence are known as the Seven Virtues:

1. Faith
2. Hope
3. Charity
4. Fortitude
5. Justice
6. Prudence
7. Temperance

The Nine Orders of Angels

According to medieval theology, there are nine orders of spiritual beings. These orders correspond to the three circles of heaven. From the highest order to the lowest, the nine orders are:

1. Seraphim
2. Cherubim
5. Virtues
6. Powers
7. Principalities
3. Thrones
4. Dominions
8. Archangels
9. Angels

Seraphim and cherubim make up the first circle of heaven, thrones and dominions the second, and virtues, powers, principalities, archangels, and angels comprise the third.

The Nine Beatitudes

In the Sermon on the Mount, Jesus preached nine beatitudes, or blessings:

1. Blessed are the poor in spirit: for theirs is the kingdom of heaven.
2. Blessed are they that mourn: for they shall be comforted.
3. Blessed are the meek: for they shall inherit the earth.
4. Blessed are they which do hunger and thirst after righteousness: for they shall be filled.
5. Blessed are the merciful: for they shall obtain mercy.
6. Blessed are the pure in heart: for they shall see God.

7. Blessed are the peacemakers: for they shall be called the children of God.

8. Blessed are they which are persecuted for righteousness' sake: for theirs is the kingdom of heaven.

9. Blessed are ye, when men shall revile you, and persecute you, and shall say all manner of evil against you falsely, for my sake. Rejoice, and be exceedingly glad: for great is your reward in heaven: for so persecuted they the prophets which were before you. (Matthew 5:3–12)

The Ten Commandments

According to Exodus, in the Old Testament, the Lord gave Moses the Ten Commandments upon two tablets. For the Anglican, Jewish, and Eastern Orthodox religions, as well as many Protestant faiths, the wording and the order are as follows:

1. I am the Lord thy God, thou shalt have no other gods before me.

2. Thou shalt not make unto thyself any graven image. . . . Thou shalt not bow down thyself to them, nor serve them.

3. Thou shalt not take the name of the Lord thy God in vain.

4. Remember the Sabbath day, to keep it holy.

5. Honor thy father and thy mother.

6. Thou shalt not kill.

7. Thou shalt not commit adultery.

8. Thou shalt not steal.

9. Thou shalt not bear false witness against thy neighbor.

10. Thou shalt not covet thy neighbor's house, thou shalt not covet thy neighbor's wife . . . nor anything that is thy neighbor's. (Exodus 20:1–17)

Moses presents the Ten Commandments

For the Roman Catholics and the Lutheran faiths, the wording and order are

1. I am the Lord thy God, thou shalt have none other gods before me.
2. Thou shalt not take the name of the Lord thy God in vain.
3. Keep holy the Sabbath day.
4. Honor thy father and thy mother.

5. Thou shalt not kill.
6. Thou shalt not commit adultery.
7. Thou shalt not steal.
8. Thou shalt not bear false witness against thy neighbor.
9. Thou shalt not covet thy neighbor's wife.
10. Thou shalt not covet thy neighbor's goods. (Deuteronomy 5:6–21)

The Twelve Apostles

The key missionaries of Christianity are:

1. Peter
2. Andrew
3. James (the Greater)
4. John
5. Thomas
6. James (the Lesser)
7. Jude (or Thaddaeus)
8. Philip
9. Bartholomew
10. Matthew
11. Simon
12. Matthias (replacing Judas Iscariot)

Paul is also considered an apostle.

The Fourteen Stations of the Cross

Fourteen episodes that occurred during the Passion of Christ are set chronologically as stations or shrines for devotions and meditation. The fourteen events are:

1. the sentencing by Pilate
2. the receiving of the Cross
3. falling the first time
4. the meeting with His mother
5. the compelling of Simon of Cyrene to carry the cross
6. the wiping of His face by Veronica
7. falling the second time
8. exhorting the women of Jerusalem
9. falling the third time
10. the stripping of His clothes
11. the crucifixion
12. His death
13. the taking down of His body from the cross
14. the burial of His body

CRIME

The Triads

Triads are Chinese secret societies that function as crime syndicates. They are responsible for most of the world's heroin and opium traffic. Their name is represented by a triangle symbolizing three basic concepts in Chinese philosophy:

1. Heaven
2. Earth
3. Man

The Five Families

This organized crime syndicate in the New York City area is composed of these families:

1. Bonanno
2. Colombo
3. Gambino
4. Genovese
5. Lucchese

Joseph (Joe Bananas) Columbo, Sr.

**Five
Iron Men** Few cities in the United States have had more Mafia corruption in government than Kansas City. In the 1930s the political machine was closely allied with mobsters. The most powerful criminal leaders came to be known as Five Iron Men:

1. Charley Binaggio, the leader, who delivered votes in the North Ward.
2. Charley Gargotta, his enforcer, was known as "mad dog."
3. Tano Lococo
4. Fat Tony Gizzo
5. Jim Balestrere

Most of the five were killed or imprisoned in the 1950s.

————

**The
Big Six** When Meyer Lansky was at the height of his powers in the 1940s and 1950s, he controlled the national crime syndicate through the Big Six. The leaders of the syndicate were:

1. Joe Adonis
2. Tony Accardo
3. Frank Costello
4. "Thumb" Guzik
5. Meyer Lansky
6. "Longy" Zwillman

————

**Seven
Group** During Prohibition mobsters devoted great energy toward killing each other and hijacking each other's shipments of scarce liquor. Gang leaders realized they were making too

little money, and so the Seven Group was formed to distribute liquor fairly and reduce the bloodshed. The seven original power groups were comprised of:

1. Joe Adonis, from Brooklyn
2. Frank and Luciano Costello, from Manhattan
3. "Waxey" Gordon, from Philadelphia
4. "Nucky" Johnson, from Atlantic City
5. Meyer Lansky and Bugsy Siegel, known as "The Enforcers"
6. Johnny "The Brain" Torrio, who is credited with the idea of forming the Seven Group.
7. "Longy" Zwillman, from New Jersey

EASTERN RELIGIONS

The Buddha of Kamakura

The Three Body Doctrine
(Buddhism)

This trinity describes the three aspects of Buddhahood. They are:

1. Transformation Body—the historical and earthly Buddhas
2. Enjoyment Body—the celestial, godlike aspects of the Buddhas
3. Truth Body—the aspect of Buddhahood identified with the Absolute

---

The Four Noble Truths
(Buddhism)

The *Dharma*, or doctrine, that the Buddha taught is summed up in these Four Noble Truths:

1. Life is filled with dissatisfaction and suffering.
2. Craving and ignorant desire is the origin of suffering.
3. The cessation of suffering is possible through the cessation of craving.
4. The way to cease suffering is through the Noble Eightfold Path.

The Four Perfect Women
(Islam)

According to Mohammed, there were four perfect women:

1. Asia, wife of Pharaoh, who raised Moses
2. Mary, daughter of Imram
3. Khadijah, Mohammed's first wife
4. Fatima, Mohammed's daughter

The Five Precepts
(Buddhism)

The five duties of all Buddhists, somewhat akin to the Ten Commandments, are rules that ban:

1. the taking of life (including animal life)
2. stealing
3. wrong sexual relations
4. wrong use of speech (such as lying and malicious gossip)
5. use of alcohol and drugs

The Five Hindrances
(Buddhism)

Buddhists believe there are five hindrances that can prevent a person from achieving enlightenment:

1. Seeking worldly advantage
2. Desiring to hurt others
3. Slackness of mind
4. Worry
5. Uncertainty of mind

The Five Duties of a Moslem
(Islam)

These duties are required of every Moslem person:

1. Profession of faith (repeating the creed daily)
2. Prayer five times a day, at designated times, facing Mecca
3. Almsgiving to the poor
4. Fasting from dawn to dusk each day during the month of Ramadan
5. Pilgrimage to Mecca once in your lifetime

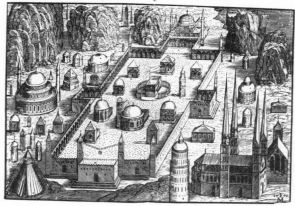

Mecca

The Six Schools of Philosophy *(Hinduism)*

Hindu philosophy encompasses six schools of practice and belief:

1. Mimamsa
2. Nyaya
3. Samkhya
4. Vaisesika
5. Vedanta
6. Yoga

The Seven Compartments of Hell *(Islam)*

In the Islamic faith, there are seven compartments to Hell, each holding a particular group of sinners:

1. Moslems
2. Jews
3. Christians
4. Sabians
5. Magians
6. Idolaters
7. Hypocrites

The Noble Eightfold Path *(Buddhism)*

The eight steps that make up the Noble Truth of the Path that Leads to the Cessation of Pain are:

1. Right view
2. Right thought
3. Right speech
4. Right action
5. Right livelihood
6. Right effort
7. Right mindfulness
8. Right concentration

EDUCATION

The Three R's

The Three R's, the naming of which is attributed to the somewhat illiterate alderman and Lord Mayor of London, Sir William Curtis (1752–1829), are:

1. Reading
2. Writing (" 'Riting")
3. Arithmetic (" 'Rithmetic")

To the above list of three R's is sometimes added a fourth, Reasoning.

———

The Trivium

The Trivium, the elementary division of studies in the Middle Ages, consisted of three of the seven liberal arts:

1. Grammar
2. Logic
3. Rhetoric

———

The Quadrivium

The Quadrivium is the second, or higher, branch of studies in the arts and sciences of the Middle Ages, taken from the four branches of Pythagorean mathematics:

1. Arithmetic
2. Astronomy
3. Geometry
4. Music

———

The Seven Sisters

The Seven Sisters are a group of women's colleges known for their academic excellence:

1. Barnard
2. Bryn Mawr
3. Mount Holyoke
4. Radcliffe

5. Smith
6. Vassar
7. Wellesley

Seals of the Seven Sisters

The Ivy League Eight Although originated as a name for the athletic league in which these academic institutions play, the term "Ivy League" is frequently used in reference to the outstanding academic reputations of the participating institutions. The eight members of the League are:

1. Brown
2. Columbia
3. Cornell
4. Dartmouth

5. Harvard
6. Princeton
7. University of Pennsylvania
8. Yale

WATERLOO

The Dual Alliance

The alliance between the following two countries from 1893 to 1917 is called the Dual Alliance. They are:

1. France
2. Russia

The Three Reichs of Germany

Germany has been governed by three reichs:

1. The Holy Roman Empire, from the ninth century to 1806
2. The German Empire, from 1871 to 1918
3. The Nazi regime, between 1933 and 1945

Battle of the Three Emperors

The decisive battle on December 2, 1805, when Napoleon defeated the Russian and Austrian armies at Austerlitz, in Moravia, Czechoslovakia, is called the Battle of the Three Emperors because three emperors were present:

1. Napoleon I of France
2. Alexander I of Russia
3. Francis I of Austria

The Triple Entente

Formed in 1907, the Triple Entente was an alliance intended to counter the Dreibund, the earlier alliance of Germany, Austria, and Italy. The three countries of the Triple Entente were:

1. France
2. Great Britain
3. Russia

The Three Kings Richard of England

1. Richard I, "the Lion-Hearted" (1157–1199). A brilliant fighter and stern ruler, he spent most of his reign leading the Third Crusade and fighting in France. He spent only six months in England, which he seemed to regard as merely a source of revenue.

The three Kings Richard: Richard I, Richard II,

2. Richard II (1367–1400). A savvy ruler who became steadily more despotic and possibly insane. He killed many of his enemies, confiscated land, and eventually starved himself to death while in prison.

3. Richard III (1452–1485). Made famous by Shakespeare as a monstrous tyrant, Richard is thought to have been a ruthless but hardworking and accessible ruler.

Richard III

The Four Estates During the middle ages in Europe, particularly in France, society was divided into three Estates of the Realm. In the last century writers adopted the term "the Fourth Estate." The four are:

1. The nobility
2. The clergy
3. The common people
4. The press

The Five Republics of France

In the tumultuous history of its modern government, France has established these republics:

1. The First Republic, 1792–1804, which was the result of the French Revolution.
2. The Second Republic, 1848–1852
3. The Third Republic, 1879–1940, which was established after the fall of Napoleon III till the German occupancy during World War II.
4. The Fourth Republic, 1946–1958
5. The Fifth Republic, which was established in 1958 when Charles de Gaulle became the president, is still in existence.

The Five Bloods

The five principal families of Ireland are known as the Five Bloods:

1. the McMurroughs of Leinster
2. the O'Briens of Thomond
3. the O'Connors of Connaught
4. the O'Lachlans of Meath
5. the O'Neils of Ulster

The Six Wives of Henry VIII

The king of England from 1491–1547, Henry VIII was married to these six women:

1. Katherine of Aragon
2. Anne Boleyn
3. Jane Seymour
4. Anne of Cleves
5. Catherine Howard
6. Catherine Parr

A famous ditty describes what happened to the six wives: divorced, beheaded, died, divorced, beheaded, survived.

The Six Kings George of England

1. George I (1660–1727). Born in Hanover in what is today Germany, this unpopular ruler was constantly accused of betraying English interests.

2. George II (1683–1760). The second member of the house of Hanover to rule England, George was also accused of sacrificing the interests of Great Britain to Hanover. However, there is no evidence that he did so.

3. George III (1738–1820). Best known in the United States for his full support of British actions that led to the American Revolution. George suffered from insanity toward the end of his life.

4. George IV (1762–1830). Hated for his dissolute and extravagant habits, the monarchy lost much power during his reign.

5. George V (1865–1936). Although a popular king, he had little impact on affairs of state.

6. George VI (1895–1952). The father of Queen Elizabeth, George gained wide popularity for his morale-boosting travels during World War II.

———

The Seven Wonders of the Middle Ages

Like their counterparts in the Ancient World, these Wonders are monuments of human achievement:

1. The Colosseum at Rome
2. The catacombs at Alexandria
3. The Great Wall of China
4. The Leaning Tower of Pisa
5. The Mosque of St. Sophia at Constantinople
6. The Porcelain Tower of Nanking
7. Stonehenge

Wonder number one: The Colosseum at Rome

The Eight Kings Edward of England

1. Edward I (1239–1307). Remembered for increasing the law-giving role of Parliament and for expelling the Jews from England in 1290.

2. Edward II (1284–1327). An extravagant, incompetent ruler, he was defeated in a war against the Scots and forced to abdicate the throne.

3. Edward III (1312–1377). A very popular ruler who won many victories in battle, his powers drastically declined in his later years.

4. Edward IV (1442–1483). A relatively peaceful monarch, he was forced to flee to France in the middle of his rule by the Earl of Warwick. The next year Edward returned and defeated Warwick.

5. Edward V (1470–1483?). A boy-king who, according to the widely believed story of Sir Thomas More, was suffocated in the Tower of London at the orders of Richard III.

6. Edward VI (1537–1553). A frail son of King Henry VIII, Edward was totally dominated by his relatives and advisors. During his rule Protestantism was established in England.

7. Edward VII (1841–1910). The eldest son of Queen Victoria, he was a highly popular king who traveled widely, enjoyed horse racing, and brought much international goodwill to England.

8. Edward III (1894–1972). The eldest son of King George V, he is best remembered for abdicating the throne after only 325 days to marry Mrs. Wallis Simpson, an American-born divorcée.

The Eight Kings Henry of England

1. Henry I (1068–1135). Also known as Henry Beauclerc, he crowned himself king while his brother, the rightful ruler, was away.

2. Henry II (1133–1189). Also known as Curtmantle, he had an argument with Thomas à Becket, the Archbishop of Canterbury, which led to Becket's murder in 1170.

3. Henry III (1207–1272). An incompetent ruler who remained in power for forty-five years.

4. Henry IV (1367–1413). Also known as Henry of Lancaster, he became king after forcing Richard II to abdicate. Henry IV suppressed several rebellions against his rule and left the crown with a huge debt.

5. Henry V (1387–1422). Remembered for winning the Battle of Agincourt in 1415. The French recognized him as heir to the throne of France.

6. Henry VI (1421–1471). Ruler during much of the Wars of the Roses, he suffered from periods of insanity and was eventually imprisoned and murdered.

7. Henry VII (1457–1509). Also known as Henry Tudor, he killed Richard III to become king. He instituted use of the Star Chamber, a court, to curb the power of the nobles.

8. Henry VIII (1491–1547). Aside from his fame as the husband of many women, Henry VIII is remembered for his break with Rome, which resulted in the creation of the Church of England.

The eighth and final Henry

The Nine Points

In heraldry, there are nine accepted places on the shield that signify the heraldic arms ("dexter" refers to the wearer's right, and therefore the observer's left; "sinister" refers to the wearer's left and the observer's right):

1. Dexter chief point
2. Chief point (upper section of the shield)
3. Sinister chief point
4. Honor point
5. Fesse (wide, horizontal band forming the midsection)
6. Nombril (between the fesse and the base point)
7. Dexter base point
8. Base point (lower section)
9. Sinister base point

The Eighteen Kings Louis of France

1. Louis I (778–840). Called "the Debonair" or "the Pious," he was the third son of Charlemagne.

2. Louis II "the Stammerer" (846–879). A son of Charles the Bald, he was a weak ruler who lost the area we today call Provence.

3. Louis III (863–882). Ruled jointly with his brother, Carloman, and recaptured Provence.

4. Louis IV (921–954). While king he was imprisoned by Hugh the Great, but returned to the throne when Otto the Great, Emperor of the Holy Roman Empire, intervened.

5. Louis V, "the Lazy" (966–987). After ruling for only one year he died suddenly when his mother poisoned him.

6. Louis VI, "the Fat" (1081–1137). The first powerful monarch of France, he created the alliance between the crown and the bourgeoisie. His twenty-year war against Henry I of England resulted in the loss of Brittany.

7. Louis VII, "the Young" (1121–1180). Responsible for a series of mistakes, including the disastrous Second Crusade and a losing war against Henry II of England.

8. Louis VIII, "the Lion" (1187–1226). Increased the power of the throne through a series of successful campaigns against the English and Albigenses, a heretical French sect.

9. Louis IX, or St. Louis (1214–1270). Brought peace and prosperity to France during his reign. He died while leading the Eighth Crusade.

10. Louis X, "the Quarrelsome" (1289–1316). The first ruler who invited serfs to buy their own freedom.

11. Louis XI (1423–1483). A skilled diplomat and administrator, he fought several wars to consolidate the power of France.

12. Louis XII, "Father of the People" (1462–1515). Captured Milan and Genoa but was later defeated during the Italian Wars.

13. Louis XIII (1601–1643). A retiring leader who exiled his mother and gave great power to Richelieu.

14. Louis XIV, "the Great" (1638–1715). Built a large centralized bureaucracy, based his absolute monarchy on the theory of divine right, and is remembered for his remark, "I am the state."

15. Louis XV, "the Well-Beloved" (1710–1774). A weak leader who fought a number of wars that nearly bankrupted the government.

Louis the XVI of France

16. Louis XVI (1754–93). With his queen, Marie Antoinette, he ignored the plight of the lower classes and was eventually guillotined during the French Revolution.

17. Louis XVII, "the lost dauphin" (1785–1795?). Claimed by some to be the figurehead ruler of France when he was imprisoned at the age of eight by revolutionists. Despite many stories that he escaped, this boy-king probably died at age ten in prison.

18. Louis XVIII (1755–1824). After being exiled he assumed the throne in 1814 and made peace with the revolutionists.

GEOGRAPHY

The Great Lakes, from an 1805 map

The Four Seas

The bodies of water that surround England are called the Four Seas, corresponding to the four major directions:

1. The Northern Sea (the North Sea)
2. The Eastern Sea (the German Ocean)
3. The Southern Sea (the English Channel)
4. The Western Sea (including the Scotch and Irish seas and St. George's Channel)

———

Four Corners

Near the town of Teec Nos Pas, Arizona, is the only place in the United States where the boundaries of four states meet. These states meet at the place called Four Corners:

1. Arizona
2. Utah
3. Colorado
4. New Mexico

———

The Five Great Lakes

This chain of lakes in the United States and Canada is comprised of:

1. Lake Superior
2. Lake Michigan

3. Lake Huron

4. Lake Erie
5. Lake Ontario

A group of five large lakes in the Great Rift Valley of eastern Africa are *also* called the Five Great Lakes. They are lakes Rudolf, Albert, Victoria, Tanganyika, and Nyasa.

The Five Tri-Cities

These five groups of towns in the United States call themselves the Tri-Cities:

1. Bristol, Johnstown City, and Kingsport, Tennessee
2. Draper, Leaksville, and Spray, North Carolina
3. Florence, Sheffield, and Tuscumbia, Alabama
4. Kennewick, Pasco, and Richland, Washington
5. Moline and Rock Island, Illinois, and Davenport, Iowa

The Six Continents

The Six Continents are:

1. Africa
2. Antarctica
3. Australia
4. Eurasia
5. North America
6. South America

Many people consider Eurasia to be two separate continents—Europe and Asia.

The Seven Seas

To sail the Seven Seas means to navigate all the major bodies of water in the world. They are:

1. The Pacific Ocean
2. The Atlantic Ocean
3. The Indian Ocean
4. The Arctic Ocean
5. The Mediterranean Sea
6. The North Sea
7. The Black seas, including the Baltic, the Aegean, and the Arabian seas

---

The Seven Hills of Rome

As its Latin name *Urbs Septicollis,* or City of Seven Hills, indicates, Rome was originally built on seven hills:

1. Aventine
2. Caeline
3. Capitoline
4. Esquiline
5. Palatine
6. Quirinal
7. Viminal

The United Arab Emirates

Composed of seven independent Arab states, the United Arab Emirates is a federated nation that lies along the eastern coast of the Arabian Peninsula. Formerly called the Trucial Oman or the Trucial States, they are:

1. Abu Dhabi
2. Ajman
3. Dubai
4. Fujairah
5. Ras al-Khaimah
6. Sharjah
7. Umm al-Qaiwain

The Ten Provinces of Canada

The Yukon Territories and the Northwest Territories along with the ten provinces make up the Dominion of Canada. The provinces are:

1. Alberta
2. British Columbia
3. Manitoba
4. New Brunswick
5. Newfoundland
6. Nova Scotia
7. Ontario
8. Prince Edward Island
9. Quebec
10. Saskatchewan

The Fifteen Soviet Republics

The Union of Soviet Socialist Republics (U.S.S.R.) is formed by:

1. Russian S.S.R.
2. Ukrainian S.S.R.
3. Uzbek S.S.R.
4. Kazakh S.S.R.

5. Byelorussian S.S.R.
6. Azerbaijan S.S.R.
7. Georgian S.S.R.
8. Tadzhik S.S.R.
9. Moldavian S.S.R.
10. Kirghiz S.S.R.
11. Lithuanian S.S.R.
12. Armenian S.S.R.
13. Turkmen S.S.R.
14. Latvian S.S.R.
15. Estonian S.S.R.

The Dodecanese

The Dodecanese are a group of fifteen Greek islands in the Aegean Sea, between Turkey and Crete. The last three islands were added to the original twelve for whom the group is named:

1. Astypalaia
2. Ikaria
3. Kalimnos
4. Karpathos
5. Kasos
6. Khalki
7. Leros
8. Lipsos
9. Nisiros
10. Patmos
11. Syme
12. Tilos
13. Kos (1912)
14. Rhodes (1912)
15. Kastellorizon (1923)

The Twenty-nine Twin Cities in the United States

All the pairs of towns below call themselves Twin Cities or the Twin City:

1. Aberdeen and Hoquiam, Washington
2. Alcoa and Maryville, Tennessee

3. Alexandria and Pineville, Louisiana
4. Auburn and Lewiston, Maine
5. Bangor and Brewer, Maine
6. Benton Harbor and St. Joseph, Michigan
7. Biddeford and Saco, Maine
8. Bloomington and Normal, Illinois
9. Bluefield, West Virginia, and Bluefield, Virginia
10. Bradenton and Sarasota, Florida
11. Bristol, Tennessee, and Bristol, Virginia
12. Central Falls and Pawtucket, Rhode Island
13. Champaign and Urbana, Illinois
14. Deadwood and Lead, North Dakota
15. Fairfield and Suison City, California
16. Gardnerville and Minden, Nevada
17. Haines and Port Chilkoot, Alaska
18. Helena and West Helena, Arkansas
19. Lafayette and West Lafayette, Indiana
20. Menasha and Neenah, Wisconsin
21. Miami and Miami Beach, Florida
22. Minneapolis and St. Paul, Minnesota
23. Monroe and West Monroe, Louisiana
24. Niceville and Valparaiso, Florida
25. Sparks and Truckee, Nevada
26. Sun City and Youngstown, Arizona
27. Texarkana, Arkansas, and Texarkana, Texas
28. Tonawanda and North Tonawanda, New York
29. Winston-Salem, North Carolina

The Fifty North American States

State	Capital	Flower	Bird
1. Alabama	Montgomery	Camellia	Yellowhammer
2. Alaska	Juneau	Forget-me-not	Willow ptarmigan
3. Arizona	Phoenix	Saguaro	Cactus wren
4. Arkansas	Little Rock	Apple blossom	Mockingbird
5. California	Sacramento	Golden poppy	California valley quail
6. Colorado	Denver	Blue columbine	Lark bunting
7. Connecticut	Hartford	Mountain laurel	Robin
8. Delaware	Dover	Peach blossom	Blue hen chicken
9. Florida	Tallahassee	Orange blossom	Mockingbird
10. Georgia	Atlanta	Cherokee rose	Brown Thrasher
11. Hawaii	Honolulu	Hibiscus	Nene goose
12. Idaho	Boise	Syringa	Mountain bluebird
13. Illinois	Springfield	Native violet	Cardinal
14. Indiana	Indianapolis	Peony	Cardinal

State	*Capital*	*Flower*	*Bird*
15. Iowa	Des Moines	Wild rose	Goldfinch
16. Kansas	Topeka	Sunflower	Western meadowlark
17. Kentucky	Frankfort	Goldenrod	Kentucky cardinal
18. Louisiana	Baton Rouge	Magnolia	Eastern brown pelican
19. Maine	Augusta	Pine cone and tassel	Chickadee
20. Maryland	Annapolis	Black-eyed susan	Baltimore oriole
21. Massachusetts	Boston	Mayflower	Chickadee
22. Michigan	Lansing	Apple	Robin
23. Minnesota	St. Paul	Showy lady slipper	Common loon
24. Mississippi	Jackson	Magnolia	Mockingbird
25. Missouri	Jefferson City	Hawthorn	Bluebird

Hawthorn

State	Capital	Flower	Bird
26. Montana	Helena	Bitterroot	Western meadowlark
27. Nebraska	Lincoln	Goldenrod	Meadowlark
28. Nevada	Carson City	Sagebrush	Mountain bluebird
29. New Hampshire	Concord	Purple lilac	Purple finch
30. New Jersey	Trenton	Purple violet	Eastern goldfinch
31. New Mexico	Santa Fe	Yucca	Roadrunner
32. New York	Albany	Rose	Bluebird

Rose (American beauty)

State	Capital	Flower	Bird
33. North Carolina	Raleigh	Dogwood	Cardinal
34. North Dakota	Bismarck	Wild prairie rose	Western meadowlark
35. Ohio	Columbus	Scarlet carnation	Cardinal

	State	Capital	Flower	Bird
36.	Oklahoma	Oklahoma City	Mistletoe	Scissor-tailed flycatcher
37.	Oregon	Salem	Oregon grape	Western meadowlark
38.	Pennsylvania	Harrisburg	Mountain laurel	Ruffed grouse
39.	Rhode Island	Providence	Violet	Rhode Island hen
40.	South Carolina	Columbia	Carolina jessamine	Carolina wren
41.	South Dakota	Pierre	Pasqueflower	Pheasant
42.	Tennessee	Nashville	Iris	Mockingbird
43.	Texas	Austin	Bluebonnet	Mockingbird
44.	Utah	Salt Lake City	Sego lily	Seagull
45.	Vermont	Montpelier	Red clover	Thrush
46.	Virginia	Richmond	Flowering dogwood	Cardinal
47.	Washington	Olympia	Rhododendron	Willow goldfinch
48.	West Virginia	Charleston	Big rhododendron	Cardinal
49.	Wisconsin	Madison	Wood violet	Robin
50.	Wyoming	Cheyenne	Indian paintbrush	Meadowlark

The 182 Countries of the World

These countries are members of the United Nations. A few of the countries that are not members do participate in specialized agencies sponsored by the U.N.

1. Afghanistan*
2. Albania*
3. Algeria*
4. Andorra*
5. Angola*
6. Antigua and Barbuda*
7. Argentina*
8. Australia*
9. Austria*
10. Bahamas*
11. Bahrain*
12. Bangladesh*
13. Barbados*
14. Belgium*
15. Belize*
16. Benin*
17. Bhutan*
18. Bolivia*
19. Botswana*
20. Brazil*
21. Brunei*
22. Bulgaria*
23. Burkina Faso*
24. Burma*
25. Burundi*
26. Cambodia*
27. Cameroon*
28. Canada*
29. Cape Verde*
30. Central African Republic*
31. Chad*
32. Chile*
33. China, People's Republic of*
34. Colombia*
35. Comoros*
36. Congo*
37. Cook Islands*
38. Costa Rica*
39. Cuba
40. Cyprus*
41. Czechoslovakia*
42. Denmark*
43. Djibouti*
44. Dominica*
45. Dominican Republic*
46. Ecuador*

47. Egypt*
48. El Salvador*
49. Equatorial Guinea*
50. Ethiopia*
51. Fiji*
52. Finland*
53. France*
54. French Guiana
55. Gabon*
56. Gambia, The*
57. German Democratic
    Republic*
58. Germany, Federal
    Republic of*
59. Ghana*
60. Greece*
61. Grenada*
62. Guadeloupe*
63. Guatemala*
64. Guinea*
65. Guinea-Bissau*
66. Guyana*
67. Haiti*
68. Honduras*
69. Hong Kong
70. Hungary*
71. Iceland*
72. India*
73. Indonesia*
74. Iran*

75. Iraq*
76. Ireland*
77. Israel*
78. Italy*

Italy

79. Ivory Coast*
80. Jamaica*
81. Japan*
82. Jordan*
83. Kenya*
84. Kiribati*
85. Korea, North*
86. Korea, South*
87. Kuwait*
88. Laos*

89. Lebanon*
90. Lesotho*
91. Liberia
92. Libya*
93. Liechtenstein*
94. Luxembourg*
95. Madagascar*
96. Malawi*
97. Malaysia*
98. Maldives*
99. Mali*
100. Malta*
101. Martinique*
102. Mauritania*
103. Mauritius*
104. Mexico*
105. Monaco
106. Mongolia*
107. Morocco*
108. Montserrat*
109. Mozambique*
110. Namibia
111. Nauru
112. Nepal*
113. Netherlands*
114. Netherlands Antilles
115. New Caledonia
116. New Zealand*
117. Nicaragua*
118. Niger*
119. Nigeria*
120. Norway*
121. Oman*
122. Pakistan*
123. Panama*
124. Papua New Guinea*
125. Paraguay*
126. Peru*
127. Philippines*
128. Poland*
129. Portugal*
130. Qatar*
131. Reunion
132. Rumania
133. Rwanda*
134. St. Christopher and Nevis*
135. St. Lucia*
136. St. Vincent and the Grenadines*
137. San Marino*
138. São Tomé and Príncipe*
139. Saudi Arabia*
140. Senegal*
141. Seychelles*
142. Sierra Leone*
143. Singapore*

144. Solomon Islands*
145. Somalia*
146. South Africa*
147. Spain*
148. Sri Lanka*
149. Sudan*
150. Surinam*
152. Swaziland*
153. Sweden*
154. Switzerland*
155. Syria*
156. Taiwan*
157. Tanzania*
158. Thailand*
159. Togo*
160. Tonga*
162. Trinidad and Tobago*
163. Tunisia*
164. Turkey*
165. Tuvalu
166. Uganda*
167. Union of Soviet
     Socialist Republics*
168. United Arab Emirates*
169. United Kingdom*
170. United States*
171. Uruguay*
172. Vanuatu*

173. Vatican City*
174. Venezuela*
175. Vietnam*
176. Western Samoa*
177. Yemen Arab Republic*
178. Yemen, People's
     Democratic Republic
     of*
179. Yugoslavia*
180. Zaire*
181. Zambia*
182. Zimbabwe*

United Kingdom

HEALTH AND THE HUMAN BODY

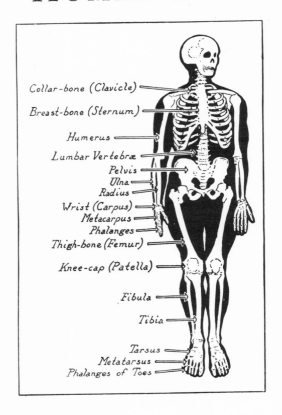

Collar-bone (Clavicle)
Breast-bone (Sternum)
Humerus
Lumbar Vertebræ
Pelvis
Ulna
Radius
Wrist (Carpus)
Metacarpus
Phalanges
Thigh-bone (Femur)
Knee-cap (Patella)
Fibula
Tibia
Tarsus
Metatarsus
Phalanges of Toes

Three Warning Signs of Breast Cancer

The National Cancer Institute recommends women give themselves a breast examination once a month. The warning signs are:

1. a lump or thickening of the breast
2. a change in breast shape
3. discharge from the nipple

The Three Stages of Labor

Labor is initiated by hormones and by the fetus, which physically stimulates the cervix. Birthing has these three phases:

1. The First Stage, in which contractions of the uterus push the fetus into the birth canal, the cervix dilates to ten centimeters, the ligaments around the pubic bones relax, and the membranes rupture.
2. The Second Stage, in which the baby is born following strong contractions of the uterus, assisted by the abdominal muscles.
3. The Third Stage, in which the placenta (afterbirth) is expelled.

The Three Layers of Skin

Although there are many sub-layers and zones, human skin has three main parts:

1. Epidermis—the outer layer
2. Dermis—the inner layer
3. Accessory organs—including sweat glands, sebaceous glands, hair, and nails

―――――

The Four Blood Types

All people have one of these major blood types:

1. A
2. B
3. O
4. AB

―――――

The Four Main Parts of a Tooth

The key parts of each tooth are:

1. Enamel; covering the entire crown, it is the hardest substance in the body.
2. Dentin, the hard, yellowish material that forms the bulk of the tooth.
3. Cementum, the thin covering of the roots
4. Pulp; found in the central cavity of the tooth, it provides nourishment to the three parts listed above.

The Four Phases of Sexual Response

Masters and Johnson and other researchers divide sexual response into these phases:

1. Excitement phase. In men, the penis becomes engorged with blood, erect, and hardened. In women, the clitoris becomes engorged with blood and the vagina becomes lubricated.
2. Plateau phase. As sexual excitement continues, blood pressure rises, heart and breathing rate increase. In men, penis circumference increases. In women, the inner two-thirds of the vagina expands and lengthens, while the outer third constricts.
3. Orgasm phase. At the height of excitement comes the release, in which men ejaculate and women experience a rhythmic contraction of the vaginal walls and clitoris. The heart and respiration rates more than double.
4. Resolution phase. Breathing returns to normal and swelling of the sex organs subsides.

The Four Primary Tastes

We taste something when our taste buds (receptors) respond to a chemical substance dissolved in saliva on the surface of our tongue. We have four types of taste buds, each responding mainly to one of the primary tastes. The tastes are:

1. Sweet, experienced mainly at the front of the tongue
2. Sour, experienced mainly at the sides of the tongue
3. Salty, experienced mainly at the front and sides of the tongue
4. Bitter, experienced mainly at the rear of the tongue

The Four Types of Headaches

Physicians diagnose headaches using these classifications:

1. Vascular headaches, which include migraines, so named because they are thought to involve abnormal functioning of blood vessels in the brain.
2. Muscle-Contraction headaches, which involve the tightening or tensing of facial and neck muscles.
3. Traction headaches, which can occur if certain parts of the head are pulled, stretched, or displaced, such as when eye muscles are tensed to compensate for eyestrain.
4. Inflammatory headaches, which can result from meningitis and diseases of the sinuses, spine, neck, ears, and teeth.

The Four Types of Teeth

Human adults normally have thirty-two teeth of these four types:

1. Incisors, located at the front of the mouth, are used for biting and grasping.

2. Cuspids, which sometimes look like fangs, are also used for biting and grasping.
3. Premolars, also known as bicuspids, are used for grinding and crushing.
4. Molars, including wisdom teeth at the back of the mouth, are also used for grinding and crushing.

Five Symptoms of Diabetes

Although there are other, less frequently noticed symptoms, the most common warning signs are:

1. Excessive thirst
2. Frequent urination
3. Weight loss
4. Fatigue
5. Alteration in vision

The Six Major Types of Diseases

There are more than 1,000 diseases that can afflict humans, but nearly all of them fall into one of these categories:

1. Bacterial diseases
2. Viral diseases
3. Fungus diseases
4. Other parasitic diseases (protozoa, worms)
5. Cancer
6. Degenerative diseases

The Six Parts of the Circulatory System

The complete system through which blood travels includes:

1. The heart—a pump
2. Arteries—which carry blood away from the heart
3. Arterioles—small arteries
4. Capillaries—tiny blood vessels throughout the tissues
5. Venules—small veins
6. Veins—which carry blood toward the heart

The Seven Warning Signs of a Stroke

A stroke occurs when the blood supply to part of the brain is cut off and that part functions improperly. You should consult a physician if you or someone nearby experiences one of these stroke warning signs, even if they are only temporary:

1. A sudden numbness or weakness of the face, arm, or leg
2. Difficulty speaking, total loss of speech, or trouble understanding others
3. Sudden dimness or loss of vision, particularly in one eye
4. Double vision
5. Unexplained headaches, or a change in the pattern of your headaches
6. Dizziness or unsteadiness
7. A recent change in personality or mental ability

The Seven Types of Bone Fractures

Most breaking or cracking of bones fit into these categories:

1. Simple fracture where the skin is not broken
2. Compound fracture where the broken bone protrudes through the skin
3. Depressed fracture, where the bone is driven inward
4. Comminuted fracture, where the bone is splintered into small fragments
5. Fatigue fracture, where the fracture is incomplete resulting from stress or strain
6. Pathological fracture, where the break is caused by disease
7. Greenstick fracture, where the fracture is incomplete and splintered; most often seen in the bones of young children

---

The Seven Primary Types of Odors

Some scientists believe that most odors can be classified into these groups:

1. Camphoraceous
2. Musky
3. Floral
4. Pepperminty
5. Etherlike
6. Pungent
7. Putrid

The Seven Warning Signs of Cancer

Cancer shows no symptoms in its beginning stages. But symptoms may appear before the disease starts to spread. Seven possible signs are:

1. unusual bleeding or discharge
2. a lump or thickening in the breast or elsewhere
3. a sore that does not heal
4. a change in bowel or bladder habits
5. hoarseness or a cough
6. indigestion or difficulty in swallowing
7. a change in a wart or mole

A person who has any of these symptoms longer than two weeks should consult a doctor promptly

---

The Body's Ten Systems

All functions and parts of the human body are part of these ten systems

1. Skeletal
2. Muscular
3. Integumentary
4. Digestive
5. Circulatory
6. Respiratory
7. Excretory
8. Nervous
9. Endocrine
10. Reproductive

The Twelve Steps of Alcoholics Anonymous

AA's Twelve Steps are a group of spiritual principles designed to remove the obsession to drink and to help the alcoholic become happy and feel more useful. These Steps have been adapted by many self-help groups. They are:

1. We admitted we were powerless over alcohol—that our lives had become unmanageable.
2. Came to believe that a Power greater than ourselves could restore us to sanity
3. Made a decision to turn our will and our lives over to the care of God as we understood Him.
4. Made a searching and fearless moral inventory of ourselves.
5. Admitted to God, to ourselves, and to another human being the exact nature of our wrongs.
6. Were entirely ready to have God remove all these defects of character.
7. Humbly asked Him to remove our shortcomings.
8. Made a list of all persons we had harmed, and became willing to make amends to them all.
9. Made direct amends to such people whenever possible, except when to do so would injure them or others.
10. Continued to take personal inventory and when we were wrong promptly admitted it.

11. Sought through prayer and meditation to improve our conscious contact with God as we understood Him, praying only for knowledge of His will for us and the power to carry that out.

12. Having had a spiritual awakening as the result of these Steps, we tried to carry this message to alcoholics, and to practice these principles in all our affairs.

The Thirteen Essential Vitamins

Certain vitamins are needed in our diet to transform foods into energy and for maintenance of our bodies. These essential vitamins are:

1. Vitamin A, or retinol, is an oil-soluble vitamin needed for new cell growth, for vision in dim light, and to prevent other eye problems.

2. Vitamin B1, or thiamine, like all the B vitamins, is water-soluble, and is required for normal digestion, growth, fertility, the normal functioning of nerve tissue, and the metabolism of carbohydrates.

3. Vitamin B2, or riboflavin, helps the body obtain energy from carbohydrates and proteins.

4. Niacin is necessary for the healthy condition of all tissue cells.

5. Pantothenic Acid is needed to support a variety of functions including growth and maintenance of the body.

6. Folic Acid, or folacin, helps the body manufacture red blood cells and in the conversion of food to energy.

7. Vitamin B6 has three forms that make proteins useful to the body and maintain body functions.

8. Vitamin B12 is necessary for the normal development of red blood cells, and the functioning of all cells, particularly in the bone marrow, nervous system, and intestines.

9. Biotin, once called vitamin H, is a member of the B-complex group needed to metabolize carbohydrates, proteins, and fats.

10. Vitamin C, or ascorbic acid, promotes growth, tissue repair, the healing of wounds, and tooth and bone formation.

11. Vitamin D aids in the absorption of calcium and phosphorus for bone formation.

12. Vitamin K is essential to blood clotting.

13. Vitamin E is an antioxidant that helps to prevent oxygen from destroying other substances, e.g., is a preservative that protects vitamin A.

Judaism

The Four Questions

At the Seder, the ceremonial feast of Passover, the youngest male child asks the Four Questions:

1. Why is this night different from all other nights?
2. On all other nights, we eat all kinds of herbs, why on this night do we eat only bitter herbs?
3. On all other nights, we do not dip our food into condiments at all, why on this night do we dip it twice?
4. On all other nights, we eat sitting upright, why on this night do we recline?

The Four Sides of the Dreidel

The dreidel, used for children's play during Hanukkah—the Festival of Lights—is a four-sided top. On each side is a different Hebrew letter. For this game, each letter represents an action:

1. *Nun* means take nothing from the pot or kitty
2. *Gimmel*, get all from the pot
3. *Heh*, get half
4. *Shin*, put some "gelt" in

As an acronym the letters stand for the sentence, "A Great Miracle Happened There." The miracle, remembered at Hanukkah, is the oil lamp that burned for eight days.

The Tetragrammaton

The tetragrammaton are the four Hebrew letters that form the name of God, transliterated as YHVH:

1. *Yod*
2. *Hey*
3. *Vav*
4. *Hey*

Since the name of God is forbidden to be pronounced, "Adonai" for "Lord" is substituted.

The Pentateuch

The first five books of the Old Testament are collectively called the Pentateuch:

1. Genesis
2. Exodus
3. Leviticus
4. Numbers
5. Deuteronomy

The Menorah

The original Menorah as described in the Old Testament (Exodus 25:31–40; 37:17–24) was a seven-branched candelabrum used in the Temple as a holy lamp. In some Jewish traditions the seven candles symbolize seven archangels:

1. Cassiel
2. Gabriel
3. Haniel
4. Madimial
5. Michael
6. Raphael
7. Zadkiel

Today, for Hanukkah, the candelabrum has nine branches, one for each of the eight nights of Hanukkah, and the ninth to be used for the *Shamash*, or lighting candle. The *shamash* must be placed apart from the other eight lights. The eight branches commemorate the miracle in the temple, when the oil for the sacred light lasted for eight days.

The Seven Forbidden Names of God

In some Jewish traditions there are seven biblical divine names used to designate God that are ineffable, that is, they may not be pronounced. These seven names are:

1. *Adonai*
2. *El*
3. *Elohim*
4. "I am that I am" (Exodus 3:14)
5. *Shaddai*
6. *YHWH*
7. *Zeba'ot*

The Ten Lost Tribes of Israel

The Ten Lost Tribes of Israel, who, unlike the other two tribes were assimilated, or "lost," are:

1. Asher
2. Dan
3. Ephraim
4. Gad
5. Issachar
6. Manasseh
7. Naphtali
8. Reuben
9. Simeon
10. Zebulon

The belief is that they will be found one day.

The Ten Plagues of Egypt

When Pharaoh would not free the Hebrew people from slavery in Egypt, in answer to Moses' plea, the Lord set ten plagues upon the Egyptians. These plagues were:

1. Blood
2. Frogs
3. Lice
4. Wild beasts
5. Blight
6. Boils
7. Hail
8. Locusts
9. Darkness
10. Slaying of the firstborn

The plagues "passed over" the Israelites. Their subsequent escape from Egypt is commemorated in the Feast of Passover.

Plague of locusts

The Thirteen Articles of Faith

The song *"Ehad Mi Yodea"* ("Who Knows One") recounts thirteen articles of Jewish faith. In each verse, one article is added, until the final verse:

Who knows thirteen? I know thirteen.

1. Thirteen are the attributes of God;
2. Twelve are the tribes of Israel;
3. Eleven were the stars in Joseph's dream;
4. Ten commandments were given on Sinai;
5. Nine is the number of the holidays;
6. Eight are the days to the service of the covenant;
7. Seven days are there in a week;
8. Six sections the Mishnah has;
9. Five books there are in the Torah;
10. Four is the number of the matriarchs;
11. Three, the number of the patriarchs;
12. Two are the tables of the commandments;
13. One is our God, in heaven and on earth.

LITERATURE

William Shakespeare

Two Gentlemen of Verona

In this play by William Shakespeare the gentlemen are two close friends who fall in love with the same woman, Silvia. They are:

1. Valentine   2. Proteus

After various adventures Valentine wins Silvia and Proteus agrees to marry his old girlfriend, Julia.

Two Noble Kinsmen

This play, written partly by Shakespeare and partly by John Fletcher, is based on Chaucer's *Knight's Tale*. The kinsmen referred to in the title are:

1. Palamon   2. Arcite

Three Lives

Gertrude Stein's first major work of fiction was a book containing three novellas. Three stories, each about a different woman, were published in 1909 under the title *Three Lives*. The stories are:

1. "The Good Anna"   3. "The Gentle Lena"
2. "Melanctha"

Three Sisters   This play, by the Russian dramatist Anton Chekhov, is set in a provincial town far from Moscow. Three of the main characters, the highly educated Prozorov sisters, long for a more exciting life. The three sisters are:

1. Olga, a teacher
2. Masha, the wife of a teacher
3. Irina, a civil servant

The Three Brontë Sisters   The three Brontë sisters were nineteenth-century novelists who originally wrote under male pseudonyms:

1. Charlotte (1816–1855), as Currer Bell
2. Emily (1818–1848), as Ellis Bell
3. Anne (1820–1849), as Acton Bell

The Three Daughters of King Lear   In Shakespeare's "King Lear" the daughters are named:

1. Goneril
2. Regan
3. Cordelia

The Three Musketeers

In Alexandre Dumas's novel *The Three Musketeers*, a Gascon who aspires to the Musketeers, D'Artagnan (sometimes numbered the fourth Musketeer), meets three of the King's Men:

1. Athos
2. Porthos
3. Aramis

The Three Musketeers

The Four Zoas This long poem by William Blake involves the warfare between four symbolic creatures, or Zoas. Identified with Blake's four fundamental aspects of Man, the four Zoas are:

1. Tharmas, the body
2. Urizen, reason
3. Luvah, emotions
4. Urthona, imagination

Four Quartets This poem by T.S. Eliot was published in four parts but was intended by the author to be a single work. The parts are:

1. "Burnt Orange" (1936))
2. "East Coker" (1940)
3. "Dry Savages" (1941)
4. "Little Gidding" (1942)

They were published as *Four Quartets* in 1944.

The Four Little Women In Louisa May Alcott's novel *Little Women*, the four sisters are:

1. Beth
2. Jo
3. Amy
4. Meg

The Five Chinese Brothers

The Five Chinese Brothers, by Claire H. Bishop and Kurt Wiese, is a children's book about five brothers, each with a different power:

1. The First Chinese Brother could swallow the sea
2. The Second Chinese Brother had an iron neck
3. The Third Chinese Brother could stretch and stretch and stretch his legs
4. The Fourth Chinese Brother could not be burned
5. The Fifth Chinese Brother could hold his breath indefinitely

---

Six Characters in Search of an Author

This 1921 play by Luigi Pirandello is about six characters who are looking for an author to dramatize their story. The six characters are:

1. The Father
2. The Stepdaughter
3. The Mother
4. The Son
5. The Boy
6. The Little Girl

The Seven Voyages of Sinbad the Sailor

Sinbad is a wealthy merchant from Baghdad who tells his story in the tenth-century folktale *The Arabian Nights' Entertainments.* During his seven voyages he:

1. visits a small island that is actually a sleeping whale.

2. obtains some diamonds and escapes from an attacking roc (a huge mythological bird).
3. encounters the Cyclops.
4. is almost buried alive.
5. kills the Old Man of the Sea.
6. visits the mountain where Adam was exiled from Eden.
7. is taken a slave by pirates but escapes.

Sinbad fights the Old Man of the Sea.

The Seven Ages of Man

In Act II, Scene vii, of *As You Like It,* Shakespeare describes seven phases of a human life.

All the world's a stage,
And all the men and women merely players:
They have their exits and their entrances;
And one man in his time plays many parts,
His acts being seven ages.

1. At first the infant, Mewling and puking in the nurse's arms
2. And then the whining school-boy . . . creeping like snail unwilling to school
3. And then the lover, sighing like a furnace . . .
4. Then a soldier, full of strange oaths, and bearded like a pard . . .
5. And the the justice . . . full of wise saws and modern instances . . .
6. The sixth age slips into the lean and slippered pantaloon with spectacles on nose and pouch on side . . .
7. Last scene of all That ends this strange eventful history, is second childishness, and mere oblivion, Sans teeth, sans eyes, sans taste, sans everything.

MILITARY

The Five Rings

Just before he died in 1645, Miyamoto Musashi, the famed Japanese painter and swordsman, wrote a book called *Go Rin No Sho*. Translated as *A Book of Five Rings*, this treatise on swordsmanship and military strategy has been adopted by business executives in Japan and elsewhere as a guide to business tactics. The five rings refer to the Five Greats ("Go Dai") of Buddhism, five key elements of the cosmos. Each of these is the subject of a chapter in *A Book of Five Rings*:

1. The Ground Book
2. The Water Book
3. The Fire Book
4. The Wind Book
5. The Book of the Void

Portrait of Miyamoto Musashi by Japanese artist, Kuniyoshi

The Five Essentials for Victory

According to *The Art of War,* by Sun Tzu, written about 500 B.C., there are five keys to victory:

1. He will win who knows when to fight and when not to fight.
2. He will win who knows how to handle both superior and inferior forces.
3. He will win whose army is animated in the same spirit throughout all ranks.
4. He will win who, prepared himself, waits to take the enemy unprepared.
5. He will win who has military capacity and is not interfered with by the sovereign.

The Five Faults of a General

According to Sun Tzu, five dangers can befall a general:

1. Recklessness, which leads to destruction
2. Cowardice, which leads to capture
3. A hasty temper that can be provoked by insults
4. A delicacy of honor that is sensitive to shame
5. Over-solicitude for his men, which exposes him to worry and trouble

MOVIES AND TELEVISION

The Marx Brothers

The Three Marx Brothers

There were originally five brothers from the Marx family who performed in vaudeville, on Broadway, and in the movies. Two of them—Gummo (real name, Milton) and Zeppo (Herbert)—did not continue performing with the other three. The three more famous Marx brothers are:

1. Chico (Leonard)
2. Groucho (Julius)
3. Harpo (Adolph)

The Three Little Pigs

This old story was developed by Walt Disney in several movies during the 1930s. The Three Little Pigs were:

1. Fifer Pig, who built his house out of straw
2. Fiddler Pig, who used wood
3. Practical Pig, who sensibly built a house out of brick

Their nemesis is, of course, the Big Bad Wolf. He has three children called the Three Little Wolves who are never named.

The Three Orphan Kittens

These Disney creations were named:

1. Fluffy
2. Muffy
3. Tuffy

The three little kittens

During the terrible blizzard they seek refuge in the house of Mammy Twoshoes. In their first movie, *The Three Orphan Kittens*, the kittens are so mischievous they are almost thrown out into the snow on several occasions. In the second film, *More Kittens*, they do get chased out but find a new home with a friendly Saint Bernard named Toliver.

Donald Duck's Three Nephews

These cheerful sons of Donald's sister, Dumbella, have appeared in Disney films since the 1930s. These nephews who are ever making "Unca Donald's" life miserable are:

1. Huey
2. Dewey
3. Louie

Three's Company This highly popular ABC half-hour comedy ran for 164 episodes from 1977 through 1984. To save money the three main characters live together. Much of the action involves their struggle to maintain their privacy and keep their relationship platonic. The three are:

1. Jack Tripper, a chef (played by John Ritter)
2. Janet Wood, a florist (Joyce DeWitt)
3. Chrissy Snow, a secretary (Suzanne Somers)

———

The Three Stooges These comedians, who specialized in violent slapstick, were active from the 1930s through the 1950s. The three were originally played by:

1. Larry Fine
2. Moe Howard
3. Jerry (Curly) Howard

The last Stooge was replaced at different times by Joe Besser, Shemp Howard, and Joe de Rita.

———

The Three Faces of Eve Joanne Woodward won an Oscar in 1958 for her portrayal of a mentally ill woman with three distinct personalities. The three "faces" are:

1. a troubled, insecure housewife

2. a sexually charged, irresponsible woman who doesn't even recognize her own child
3. a healthy, educated, and relatively sophisticated combination of the first two who finally emerges

---

My Three Sons

This long-running TV sitcom starred Fred MacMurray, playing the part of Steve Douglass, a widower who is bringing up his three sons. In the original cast William Frawley played the grandfather, Bub O'Casey, who does the housekeeping. He was later replaced by William Demarest, playing Uncle Charlie O'Casey. The three sons were:

1. Mike (played by Tim Considine)
2. Robbie (Don Grady)
3. Chip (Stanley Livingston)

When Mike got married and was written out of the script, he was replaced by Ernie, an adopted son.

---

121 Movies Whose Titles Begin with Three

1. *Three*
2. *Three Bad Men in the Hidden Fortress*
3. *Three Bad Sisters*
4. *Three Bites of the Apple*

5. *Three Blind Mice*
6. *Three Blondes in His Life*
7. *Three Brave Men*
8. *Three Broadway Girls*
9. *Three Brothers*
10. *The Three Caballeros*
11. *Three Came Home*
12. *Three Came to Kill*
13. *Three Card Monte*
14. *Three Cases of Murder*
15. *Three Cheers for Love*
16. *Three Cheers for the Irish*
17. *Three Cockeyed Sailors*
18. *Three Coins in the Fountain*
19. *Three Comrades*
20. *Three-Cornered Hat*
21. *Three Crooked Men*
22. *Three Daring Daughters*
23. *Three Days of the Condor*
24. *Three Days of Viktor Tschernikoff*
25. *Three Desperate Men*
26. *Three Dolls from Hong Kong*
27. *Three Fables of Love*
28. *Three Faces East*
29. *Three Faces of a Woman*
30. *The Three Faces of Eve*
31. *Three Faces of Sin*
32. *Three Faces West*
33. *Three for Bedroom C*
34. *Three for Jamie Dawn*

35. *Three for the Show*
36. *Three Girls About Town*
37. *Three Girls Lost*
38. *Three Godfathers*

John Wayne acted in four movies whose titles begin with "Three." They are listed here at numbers 32, 37, 38, and 103.

39. *Three Guns for Texas*
40. *Three Guys Named Mike*
41. *Three Hats for Lisa*
42. *Three Hearts for Julia*
43. *Three Hours*
44. *Three Hours to Kill*
45. *Three Husbands*

46. *Three in One*
47. *Three in the Attic*
48. *Three in the Saddle*
49. *Three into Two Won't Go*
50. *Three Is a Family*
51. *Three Kids and a Queen*
52. *The Three Legionnaires*
53. *Three Little Girls in Blue*
54. *Three Little Sisters*
55. *Three Little Words*
56. *Three Live Ghosts*
57. *The Three Lives of Thomasina*
58. *Three Loves Has Nancy*
59. *Three Married Men*
60. *Three Men and a Baby*
61. *Three Men from Texas*
62. *Three Men in a Boat*
63. *Three Men in White*
64. *Three Men on a Horse*
65. *Three Men to Destroy*
66. *The Three Mesquiteers*
67. *Three Moves to Freedom*
68. *Three Musketeers (four versions)*
69. *Three Nights of Love*
70. *Three Nuts in Search of a Bolt*
71. *Three of a Kind*
72. *Three on a Couch*
73. *Three on a Honeymoon*
74. *Three on a Match*
75. *Three on a Spree*

76. *Three on a Ticket*
77. *Three on the Trail*
78. *The Three Outlaws*
79. *Three Penny Opera*
80. *Three Ring Circus*
81. *Three Rogues*
82. *Three Russian Girls*
83. *Three Sailors and a Girl*
84. *Three Secrets*
85. *Three Shades of Love*
86. *Three Silent Men*
87. *The Three Sisters (four versions)*
88. *Three Smart Girls*
89. *Three Smart Girls Grow Up*
90. *Three Sons*
91. *Three Sons O'Guns*
92. *Three Spare Wives*
93. *Three Steps in the Dark*
94. *Three Steps North*
95. *Three Stooges Go Around the World in a Daze*
96. *The Three Stooges in Orbit*
97. *The Three Stooges Meet Hercules*
98. *Three Stooges vs. Wonder Woman*
99. *Three Strangers*
100. *Three Stripes in the Sun*
101. *Three Sundays to Live*
102. *Three Tales of Chekhov*
103. *Three Texas Steers*
104. *Three the Hard Way*
105. *Three to Home*

Close Encounters of the Third Kind

In this 1976 Steven Spielberg film, starring Richard Dreyfuss, François Truffaut, and Teri Garr, the three types of encounters are:

1. Sighting the aliens
2. Physical evidence left by the aliens
3. Actual, close-up contact with the aliens

Four Versions of The Three Musketeers

Based on the famous novel by Alexandre Dumas, the first version of this film was a silent movie starring Douglas Fairbanks (1921). There have been four versions since starring:

1. Walter Abel (playing D'Artagnan), Paul Lukas (Athos), Moroni Olsen (Portos), and Onslow Stevens (Aramis), made in 1935.
2. Don Ameche (D'Artagnan), Douglas Dumbrille (Athos), Russell Hicks (Portos), and John King (Aramis), made in 1939.
3. Gene Kelly (D'Artagnan), Van Heflin (Athos), Gil Young (Portos), and Robert Coote (Aramis), made in 1948.
4. Michael York (D'Artagnan), Oliver Reed (Athos), Frank Findlay (Portos), and Richard Chamberlain (Aramis), made in 1974. In 1975 a sequel, *The Four Musketeers*, was shown with the same cast from the 1974 version.

The Seven Dwarfs

Snow White and the Seven Dwarfs has enchanted audiences for over fifty years. The Seven Dwarfs are:

1. Dopey, the most popular dwarf, who is youthful and irresponsible.
2. Doc, the leader, known for mangling the English language.

3. Grumpy, who is hostile, paranoid, and particularly suspicious of women.
4. Happy, who is always smiling and has the smallest role in the film.
5. Sleepy, who has such powers to doze off, a fly that lands on his nose also falls asleep.
6. Bashful, who giggles shyly whenever anyone notices him.
7. Sneezy, who can produce a sneeze of such power it throws his six companions across the room.

Other dwarf names considered and rejected by the Disney studio included Baldy, Biggo-Ego, Burpy, Gabby, Jumpy, Nifty, Puffy, Stubby, Stuffy, and Wheezy.

The Seven Samurai

Thought by many critics to be one of the finest movies ever made, *The Seven Samurai* was directed by Akira Kurasawa and released in 1956. It portrays a group of warriors who defend a Japanese village in the 1600s. The Seven are:

1. Kambei, Leader of the Samurai (played by Takashi Shimura)
2. Kikuchiyo, Would-Be Samurai (Toshiro Mifune)
3. Gorobei, Wise Warrior (Yoshio Inaba)
4. Kyuzo, Swordsman (Seiji Miyaguchi)
5. Heihachi, Good-Natured Samurai (Minoru Chiaki)
6. Shichiroji, Kambei's Friend (Daisuke Kato)
7. Katsushiro, Young Samurai (Ko Kimura)

The Magnificent Seven

In 1960 John Sturges made an Americanized version of *The Seven Samurai*. In this western, called *The Magnificent Seven,* seven gunslingers are hired to protect a Mexican village besieged by cutthroats. The Seven are:

1. Yul Brenner (as Chris)
2. Steve McQueen (Vin)
3. Charles Bronson (O'Reilly)
4. Horst Buchholz (Chico)
5. Robert Vaughn (Lee)
6. Brad Dexter (Harry Luck)
7. James Coburn (Britt)

Eight Is Enough This 60-minute comedy-drama ran for 112 episodes on ABC from 1977 through 1981. It chronicles the daily lives of the Bradford family living in Sacramento, California. The father, Tom Bradford, is a newspaper columnist played by Dick Van Patten. His wife, Joan Bradford, is played by Diana Hyland. When she dies Tom's second wife is played by Betty Buckley. The parents agree that their eight children are more than enough. The kids are:

1. Mary (played by Lani O'Grady)
2. Joanie (Laurie Walters)
3. Nancy (Kimberly Beck; Dianne Kay)
4. Elizabeth (Connie Needham)
5. Susan (Susan Richardson)
6. David (Mark Hamil; Grant Goodeve)
7. Tommy (Chris English; Willie Aimes)
8. Nicholas (Adam Rich)

––––––––

Twelve Angry Men In this 1957 film twelve jurors retire to a hot, humid courtroom in New York City to decide the fate of a teenager accused of killing his father with a knife. The first vote is 11 to 1 in favor of a guilty verdict. Only Henry Fonda's character believes that there is reasonable doubt. Eventually he wins the others over to his opinion. The twelve jurors are:

Juror #1 (played by Martin Balsam)
Juror #2 (John Fiedler)
Juror #3 (Lee J. Cobb)

Juror #4 (E. G. Marshall)
Juror #5 (Jack Klugman)
Juror #6 (Edward Binns)
Juror #7 (Jack Warden)
Juror #8 (Henry Fonda)
Juror #9 (Joseph Sweeney)
Juror #10 (Ed Begley)
Juror #11 (George Voskovec)
Juror #12 (Robert Webber)

———

The Dirty Dozen

In this extremely violent film, Lee Marvin, playing the role of Major Reisman, leads twelve felons on an impossible mission—to attack a heavily fortified chateau in Nazi Germany. Only three return alive. The criminals who form the dozen are:

1. Charles Bronson (as Joseph Wladislaw)
2. Jim Brown (Robert Jefferson)
3. Tom Busby (Milo Vladek)
4. Ben Carruthers (Glenn Gilpin)
5. John Cassavetes (Victor Franko)
6. Stuart Cooper (Roscoe Lever)
7. Trini Lopez (Pedro Jiminez)
8. Colin Maitland (Seth Sawyer)
9. Al Mancini (Tassos Bravos)
10. Telly Savalas (Archer Maggott)
11. Donald Sutherland (Vernon Pinkley)
12. Clint Walker (Samson Posey)

The Twenty-three Categories of the Academy Awards

Oscars are awarded each year for the best in these categories:

1. Film
2. Foreign-Language Film
3. Director
4. Actor
5. Actress
6. Supporting Actor
7. Supporting Actress
8. Original Screenplay
9. Screenplay Adaption
10. Cinematography
11. Editing
12. Original Score
13. Original Song
14. Art Direction
15. Costume Design
16. Sound
17. Sound Editing
18. Makeup
19. Visual Effects
20. Documentary, Feature
21. Documentary, Short Subject
22. Short Film, Animated
23. Short Film, Live

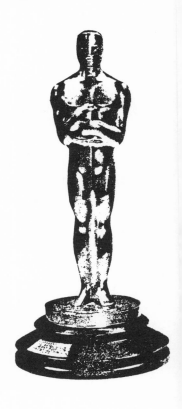

Most years at least one other special award is given. In 1990 there were three: an Honorary Award, the Jean Hersholt Humanitarian Award, and the Gordon E. Sawyer Technical Award.

The Thirty-seven Mouseketeers

The "Mickey Mouse Club" television show, from Walt Disney Productions, had its first run from 1955–1959 and was later seen in reruns during the 1960s and 1970s. The children who appeared on every show were called the Mouseketeers. They were:

The Red Team

1. Sharon Baird
2. Bobby Burgess
3. Lonnie Burr
4. Tommy Cole
5. Annette Funicello
6. Darlene Gillespie
7. Cheryl Holdridge
8. Cubby O'Brien
9. Karen Pendleton
10. Doreen Tracey

The Blue Team

11. Don Agrati
12. Sherry Allen
13. Nancy Abbate
14. Billie Beanblossom
15. Johnny Crawford
16. Dennis Day
17. Eileen Diamond
18. Dickie Dodd
19. Mary Espinosa
20. Bonnie Lynn Fields
21. Judy Harriet
22. Linda Hughes
23. Dallas Johann
24. Lee Johann

25. Bonnie Kern
26. Charles Laney
27. Larry Larson
28. Paul Peterson
29. Lynn Ready
30. Mary Lynn Sartori

31. Bronxon Scott
32. Michael Smith
33. Jay Jay Solari
34. Ronald Steiner
35. Margene Storey
36. Mark Sutherland
37. Don Underhill

MUSIC AND THE ARTS

Johann Sebastian Bach

The Three Types of Greek Columns

Classical Greek architecture used these three types of columns:

1. Doric
2. Ionic
3. Corinthian

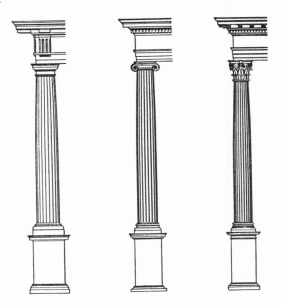

The ancient Romans added the Tuscan and Composite styles of columns to this list.

The Three Degrees

Popular in the mid-1960s through the mid-1970s, this trio is best remembered for their song "When Will I See You Again."
The members were:

1. Fayette Pinkney
2. Linda Turner, replaced by Sheila Ferguson
3. Shirley Porter, replaced by Valerie Holiday

The Kingston Trio

Known for singing "Tom Dooley" (1958) and "Where Have All the Flowers Gone" (1962), The Kingston Trio consisted of:

1. Bob Shane
2. Nick Reynolds
3. Dave Guard

The Fab Four

They were originally called the Quarrymen, the Moonshiners, Johnny and the Moon Dogs, and Long John and the Silver Beatles. By 1962 the group settled on calling themselves the Beatles. The members were:

1. John Winston Lennon
2. James Paul McCartney
3. George Harrison
4. Ringo Starr (Richard Starkey), who replaced Peter Best

A fifth Beatle, guitar player Stuart Sutcliffe, died in 1962.

The Four Seasons

This group was wildly popular in the 1960s and launched a successful solo career for Frankie Valli. Their best-known hits included: "Sherry," "Walk Like a Man," "Candy Girl," "Rag Doll," and "Let's Hang On." The Four Seasons were:

1. Frankie Valli
2. Tommy De Vito
3. Bob Gaudio
4. Nick Massi

The Four Tops

The Four Tops were one of several male vocal groups who recorded for Motown Records in the 1960s. Their hits included "Baby, I Need Your Loving," "Reach Out," and "I'll Be There." The Four Tops are:

1. Levi Stubbs
2. Abdul "Duke" Fakir
3. Renaldo "Obie" Benson
4. Lawrence Payton, Jr.

The Five Satins

Best known for their 1956 hit "In the Still of the Night," the members of the Five Satins were:

1. Fred Parris, lead singer
2. Rich Freeman, tenor
3. West Forbes, second tenor
4. Lewis Peeples, harmony
5. Sy Hopkins, bass

The Dave Clark Five

In the 1960s this British group enjoyed wide popularity in the United States with such songs as "Catch Us If You Can." The members were:

1. Dave Clark, drums
2. Lenny Davidson, guitar
3. Rick Huxley, bass
4. Denis Payton, tenor sax
5. Michael Smith, lead vocals, keyboards

The Jackson Five

One of the most popular groups in history, The Jackson Five originally consisted of:

1. Michael Joe Jackson
2. Marlon David Jackson

3. Jermaine LaJuane Jackson
4. Toriano Adaryll (Tito) Jackson
5. Sigmund Esco (Jackie) Jackson

In 1975 three other family members were added to the group: Randy Jackson, LaToya Jackson, and Maureen Jackson Brown.

———

The Five Blessings

In Chinese art, the Five Blessings, symbolized as bats, are:

1. Serenity
2. Virtue
3. Wealth
4. Longevity
5. Easy Death

———

The Russian Five

The national school of Russian music was formed about 1875 through the efforts of five Russian composers:

1. Mily A. Balakirev (1837–1910)
2. Aleksandr P. Borodin (1833–87)
3. Cesar A. Cui (1835–1918)
4. Modest P. Mussorgsky (1839–1881)
5. Nikolai A. Rimsky-Korsakov (1844–1908)

The Five Positions in Ballet

These five positions of the feet are fundamental to all classical ballet. The positions are the starting and ending points for ballet movements. They are:

1. First position, in which the heels are together, toes turned out so the feet are in a straight line.
2. Second position, in which the feet are about twelve inches apart, turned outward in a parallel line, the weight equally distributed.
3. Third position, in which the heel of one foot rests against the instep of the other, both feet turned out.
4. Fourth position, in which one foot rests about twelve inches in front of the other, both turned out, with the weight evenly distributed.
5. Fifth position, in which the feet are turned out and pressed closely together, the heel of one foot against the toe of the other.

Les Six

Named by French music critic Henry Collet, Lex Six were six French musicians and composers in the 1920s. Promoted by Jean Cocteau, they turned the course of French music away from Wagnerian Romanticism and Debussy's Impressionism. They were:

1. Georges Auric (1899–1983)
2. Louis Durey (1888–1979)

3. Arthur Honegger (1892–1955)
4. Darius Milhaud (1892–1974)
5. Francis Poulenc (1899–1983)
6. Germaine Tailleferre (1892–1983)

The Six Essentials in Painting

Ching Hao, a tenth-century Chinese artist, describes Six Essentials to painting in his *Notes on Brushwork:*

1. Spirit
2. Rhythm
3. Thought
4. Scenery
5. Brush
6. Ink

Bach's Six Brandenburg Concerti

Named after the Margrave Christian Ludwig of Brandenburg for whom J. S. Bach once worked, these concerti are Bach's most popular compositions. They are:

1. Concerto No. 1, in the key of F, unusual in that it calls for a violino piccolo, a tiny violin
2. Concerto No. 2, in F, unusual in its use of four high-pitched instruments
3. Concerto No. 3, in G

4. Concerto No. 4, in G
5. Concerto No. 5, in D
6. Concerto No. 6, in B flat, essentially a concerto for two violas

---

The Eight   In New York City in 1908, a group of American artists exhibited their realistic paintings together. They were rebelling against the traditional academic aesthetics of European artistic convention. The Eight were:

1. Arthur B. Davies
2. William J. Glackens
3. Robert Henri
4. Ernest Lawson
5. George Luks
6. Maurice Prendergast
7. Everett Shinn
8. John Sloan

The Eight Notes of the Musical Scale   The most common scale in Western music, the diatonic scale, has these eight notes in the key of C major:

1. C (Do)
2. D (Re)
3. E (Me)
4. F (Fa)
5. G (So)
6. A (La)
7. B (Ti)
8. C (Do)

Beethoven's Nine Symphonies

These compositions, the most famous written by Beethoven, are the:

Ludwig von Beethoven

1. Symphony No. 1 in C Major, Opus 21
2. Symphony No. 2 in D Major, Opus 36
3. Symphony No. 3 in E-Flat Major, Opus 55, "The Eroica"
5. Symphony No. 4 in B-Flat Major, Opus 69
5. Symphony No. 5 in C Minor, Opus 67
6. Symphony No. 6 in F Major, Opus 68, "The Pastoral"
7. Symphony No. 7 in A Major, Opus 92
8. Symphony No. 8 in F Major, Opus 93
9. Symphony No. 9 in D Minor, Opus 125, "The Choral"

The Ten American Painters

In 1898, ten American painters formed a group who exhibited together as a way of highlighting their work:

1. Frank W. Benson
2. Joseph De Camp
3. Thomas W. Dewing
4. Childe Hassam
5. Willard Leroy Metcalf
6. Robert Reid
7. E. E. Simmons
8. Edmund Charles Tarbell
9. John Henry Twachtman
10. J. Alden Weir

William Merritt Chase was added when Twachtman died in 1902.

MYTHOLOGY AND
ANCIENT HISTORY

Temple of Poseidon, Paestum, Greece (c. 460 B.C.)

The Twins

Also known as the Dioscuri, these mythological figures are named:

1. Castor, the son of Leda and Tyndareaus; he excelled as a horseman.
2. Pollux, the son of Leda and Zeus; he excelled as a boxer.

The Two Pillars of Hercules

The two head lands that guard the eastern end of the Strait of Gibraltar are called the Pillars of Hercules. They are the:

1. Rock of Gibraltar
2. Jubal Musa

According to the legend, Hercules tore apart a single rock to form these two promontories.

The First Triumvirate

The Triumvirate was a group of three men who together governed in ancient Rome. The First Triumvirate, in 60 B.C., was composed of:

1. Crassus
2. Julius Caesar
3. Pompeii

The Second Triumvirate

The Second Triumvirate, which ruled in 43 B.C., was the Roman governing coalition of:

1. Lepidus
2. Mark Antony
3. Octavian Augustus

The Three Cyclopes

Their single eyes centered in their foreheads, the Three Cyclopes were one-eyed Titans—children of Uranus and Gaea—who forged thunderbolts for Zeus. They also forged Pluto's helmet and Poseidon's trident. Their names were:

1. Arges
2. Brontes
3. Steropes

The Three Fates

Also known as the Moirae, the Three Fates of Greek mythology controlled human destiny. They were:

1. Clotho, who spun the thread of life
2. Lachesis, who measured it
3. Atropos, who cut it

In Roman mythology, they were known as the Parcae.

The Three Furies

Terrifying in appearance, the Three Furies were goddesses who pursued and punished those who were guilty of crimes but who had escaped retribution. Also known as the Eumenides or the Erinyes, they were named:

1. Alecto
2. Magaera

3. Tisephone

The Three Graces

These three brought charm and beauty to nature and to human life. They were named:

1. Aglaia (meaning bright or splendid)
2. Euphrosyne (mirth or cheerful)
3. Thalia (bloom)

The Three Harpies

The Harpies were loathsome and horrible creatures, with the heads and torsos of women, and the tail, wings, and talons of birds. Virgil refers to three of them:

1. Aello
2. Ocypete

3. Celeno

The Three Muses

The Three Muses, patron goddesses of the arts, were named:

1. Aoide, the Muse of Song
2. Melete, the Muse of Meditation
3. Mneme, the Muse of Remembrance

The Three Sirens

These sea nymphs sang so beautifully that sailors who heard them were mesmerized and shipwrecked. Jason and the Argonauts and also Odysseus were the only sailors who avoided the spell of the three Sirens. They were named:

1. Leucosia
2. Ligea
3. Parthenope

The Five Adoptive Emperors

Together, five successive emperors of Rome are called The Adoptive Emperors because each one was the adopted son of the emperor who came before him. These rulers were:

1. Nerva (A.D. 96–98)
2. Trajan (A.D. 98–117)
3. Hadrian (A.D. 117–138)
4. Antonius Pius (A.D. 138–161)
5. Marcus Aurelius (A.D. 161–180)

Seven Against Thebes

In Greek legend there were seven heroes who made war against Eteocles, the king of Thebes. These Seven Against Thebes were:

1. Polynices
2. Adrastus
3. Amphiaraus
4. Hippomedon
5. Capaneus
6. Tydeus
7. Parthenopaeus

The plays *Seven Against Thebes* by Aeschylus and Euripides' *Phoenician Women* are based on this story.

Seven Wonders of the Ancient World

Seven awe-inspiring monuments of human achievement in antiquity comprise the Wonders of the Ancient World. They are the:

1. Egyptian pyramids
2. Colossus at Rhodes
3. Hanging gardens of Babylon
4. Lighthouse on Pharos at Alexandria
5. Phidias's statue of Zeus at Olympia
6. Tomb of Mausolus at Halicarnassus
7. Temple of Artemis at Ephesus

Only the pyramids are still standing today.

Wonder number six: The tomb of Mausolus at Halicarnassus

The Nine Gods of the Sabines

The Novensiles, the Nine Gods of the Sabines (an ancient tribe of Italy), were:

1. Aeneas
2. Bacchus
3. Esculapius
4. Fides
5. Fortuna
6. Hercules
7. Romulus
8. Santa
9. Vesta

The Nine Muses

Daughters of Mnemosyne and Zeus, the Nine Muses each were responsible for a different art or science. They are:

1. Calliope, Muse of epic poetry
2. Clio, Muse of history
3. Erato, Muse of erotic or love poetry
4. Euterpe, Muse of lyric poetry
5. Melpomene, Muse of tragedy
6. Polyhymnia, Muse of sacred poetry
7. Terpsichore, Muse of dance
8. Thalia, Muse of comedy
9. Urania, Muse of astronomy

The Nine Worthies

The Nine Worthies are famous individuals whose importance make them comparable to the Seven Wonders of the Ancient World. They are commonly grouped in threes, as Gentiles, Jews, and Christians. The Nine Worthies are:

1. Alexander
2. Hector
3. Julius Caesar
4. Joshua
5. David
6. Judas Maccabaeus
7. King Arthur
8. Charlemagne
9. Godfrey of Bouillon

The Decapolis

About 62 or 63 B.C. the Decapolis, a federation of ten Greek cities in the northeastern part of ancient Palestine, was established. The ten cities were:

1. Abilia
2. Canatha
3. Damascus
4. Dium
5. Gadara
6. Gerasa
7. Hippos
8. Pella
9. Philadelphia
10. Scythopolis

The Asir

The Asir, the twelve chief gods of Norse mythology, are:

1. Odin
2. Thor
3. Bragi
4. Tyr
5. Frey
6. Heimdall
7. Baldr
8. Niord
9. Porset
10. Ullur
11. Vali
12. Vidar

The Twelve Knights of the Round Table

In Arthurian legend there is no one definitive list of the Twelve Knights of the Round Table. According to Dryden these are the twelve:

1. Lancelot
2. Tristam
3. Lamoracke

4. Tor
5. Galahad
6. Gawain
7. Gareth
8. Palomides
9. Kay
10. Mark
11. Mordred
12. and another who may be named Ector de Maris, Ewain, Gaheris, Lionel, Pelleas, Percival, or one of several others

---

The Twelve Labors of Hercules

According to Greco-Roman myth, Hercules was given twelve seemingly impossible tasks to complete by Eurystheus, to whom he was subject. He completed these twelve "labors":

1. Bringing back the skin of the Nemean lion
2. Killing the Lernean Hydra (the nine-headed monster)
3. Capturing the Arcadian Hind (a stag)
4. Capturing the Erymanthean Boar
5. Cleaning the Augean Stables in a single day
6. Killing the Stymphalian Birds
7. Capturing the Minotaur
8. Capturing the Diomedan Mares
9. Obtaining the Girdle of Hippolyte (who was Queen of the Amazons)
10. Seizing the Oxen of Geryon
11. Bringing back the Golden Apples of Hesperides
12. Bringing Cerberus up from Hades

Labor number two: Hercules fighting the Lernean Hydra

The Twelve Olympians

The twelve principal gods who lived on Mt. Olympus were:

1. Zeus
2. Poseidon
3. Aphrodite
4. Apollo
5. Ares
6. Artemis
7. Athena
8. Demeter
9. Dionysus
10. Hephaestus
11. Hera
12. Hermes

The Twelve Titans

The Titans were the primordial gods, children of Uranus and Gaea, who were overthrown by Zeus. There were six male and six female Titans:

1. Coeus
2. Crius
3. Hyperion
4. Iapetus
5. Kronos
6. Oceanus
7. Mnemosyne
8. Phoebe
9. Rhea
10. Tethis
11. Theia
12. Themis

New Age

Rudolf Steiner

The Four Etheric Formative Forces

Rudolf Steiner first detailed these forces in an optics course in 1921. Based on the ancient concept of Ether, Steiner tried to explain them as forces streaming in from the cosmos that cannot be perceived by our senses but whose effects can be studied. These forces are embodied in each person and in all matter. The four are:

1. Warm Ether, which causes hot or fiery conditions and appears in the color red.
2. Light Ether, which causes gaseous and airy conditions and appears in yellow.
3. Chemical Ether, which causes fluid or watery conditions and appears in blue.
4. Life Ether, which causes solid or earthly conditions and appears in violet.

The Six Senses

Several writers attempting to explain paranormal phenomena have suggested that there is a sixth sense beyond the conventional five. The six are:

1. sight
2. hearing
3. smell
4. taste
5. touch
6. clairvoyance

The Seven Principles of Man

According to the teachings of Theosophy, actually based on Hindu beliefs, a human being can have seven parts of being, or Principles:

1. *Atman,* the universal self
2. *Buddhi,* the intellectual principle
3. *Manas,* the mental principle
4. *Kama,* desire
5. *Prana,* subtle vitality
6. *Linga-sarira,* astral body
7. *Sthula-sarira,* physical matter

The Seven Principles of Spiritualism

Although spiritualists have no official creed, the Spiritualist's National Union has adopted these Seven Principles:

1. The Fatherhood of God
2. The Brotherhood of Man
3. The Communion of Spirits and the Ministry of Angels
4. The Continuous Existence of the Human Soul
5. Personal Responsibility
6. Compensation and Retribution hereafter for all the good and evil deeds done on earth
7. Eternal progress open to every soul

Twelve Signs of the Zodiac

The zodiac is the band in the sky about nine degrees on either side of the ecliptic, through which the sun, moon, and several planets appear to travel. Two thousand years ago the Greeks divided this band into twelve parts, each thirty degrees wide, and called it the zodiac. The corresponding constellations are:

Sign	Dates	Planet	Element
1. Aries (the Ram)	Mar. 21–Apr. 19	Mars	fire
2. Taurus (the Bull)	Apr. 20–May 20	Venus	earth
3. Gemini (the Twins)	May 21–June 21	Mercury	air
4. Cancer (the Crab)	June 22–July 22	Moon	water
5. Leo (the Lion)	July 23–Aug. 22	Sun	fire
6. Virgo (the Virgin)	Aug. 23–Sept. 22	Mercury	earth
7. Libra (the Balance)	Sept. 23–Oct. 23	Venus	air
8. Scorpius (the Scorpion)	Oct. 24–Nov. 21	Mars	water
9. Sagittarius (the Archer)	Nov. 22–Dec. 21	Jupiter	fire
10. Capricornus (the Goat)	Dec. 22–Jan. 19	Saturn	earth
11. Aquarius (the Water Bearer)	Jan. 20–Feb. 18	Uranus	air
12. Pisces (the Fishes)	Feb. 19–Mar. 20	Neptune	water

The Twelve Senses

Some writers believe there are twelve senses that are spiritually connected with the twelve constellations. They are:

1. Sense of touch
2. Sense of life
3. Sense of movement
4. Sense of balance
5. Sense of smell
6. Sense of taste
7. Sense of sight
8. Sense of warmth
9. Sense of hearing
10. Sense of speech
11. Sense of thought
12. Sense of ego

———

The Major Arcana

In the original seventy-two-card tarot deck used for fortune telling, the Major Arcana are the twenty-two picture cards (numbering and value may vary):

1. The Magician
2. The High Priestess
3. The Empress
4. The Emperor
5. The Hierophant (interpreter of sacred mysteries)
6. The Lovers
7. The Chariot
8. Justice (sometimes Strength)
9. The Hermit
10. The Wheel of Fortune
11. Strength (sometimes Justice)

12. The Hanged Man
13. Death
14. Temperance
15. The Devil
16. The Tower
17. The Star
18. The Moon
19. The Sun
20. The (Last) Judgment
21. The World
22. The Fool (sometimes numbered first, or given no value)

LE · DIABLE

LA · MAISON · DIEU

ORGANIZATIONS

The Four-H Club

This organization, sponsored by the United States Department of Agriculture, works in rural communities to teach farming methods to young people. The aim of the organization is to improve:

1. Head
2. Heart

3. Hands
4. Health

The Group of Seven

The Group of Seven is a committee formed by the finance ministers of seven countries that meet to discuss and establish international economic strategies, foreign exchange rates, and other monetary policies. The seven countries represented are:

1. Canada
2. France
3. Great Britain
4. Italy

5. Japan
6. United States
7. West Germany

The Seven Nations of the Warsaw Pact

This mutual-defense alliance was created in 1955. In 1990 the members are:

1. Bulgaria
2. Czechoslovakia
3. East Germany
4. Hungary

5. Poland
6. Romania
7. U.S.S.R.

The Twelve Common Market Countries

Founded in 1958, the Common Market is an economic union, officially named the European Economic Community, formed among western European nations. The original members numbered six; currently, there are twelve countries associated with it:

1. Belgium (1958)
2. France (1958)
3. Italy (1958)
4. Luxembourg (1958)
5. Netherlands (1958)
6. West Germany (1958)
7. Denmark (1973)
8. Ireland (1973)
9. United Kingdom (1973)
10. Greece (1981)
11. Portugal (1986)
12. Spain (1986)

The Thirteen Nations of OPEC

The Organization of Petroleum Exporting Countries (OPEC) was formed in 1960 in order to influence oil pricing and production. These thirteen oil producers are:

1. Algeria
2. Ecuador
3. Gabon
4. Indonesia
5. Iran
6. Iraq
7. Kuwait
8. Libya
9. Nigeria
10. Qatar
11. Saudi Arabia
12. United Arab Emirates
13. Venezuela

The Sixteen NATO Nations

The North Atlantic Treaty Organization was created in 1949 for mutual defense. If a country is attacked the others consider themselves also under attack. In 1990 the NATO countries are:

1. Belgium
2. Canada
3. Denmark
4. France
5. Greece
6. Iceland
7. Italy
8. Luxembourg
9. Netherlands
10. Norway
11. Portugal
12. Spain
13. Turkey
14. United Kingdom
15. United States
16. West Germany

PHILOSOPHY

Aristotle

The Threefold Aim of Art

Aristotle believed there were three goals in artistic creation:

1. To induce relaxation and pleasure
2. To achieve purification of the soul, which leads to
3. Moral perfection

The Three Keys to Happiness at Work

According to John Ruskin (1819–1900), three things are needed to make people happy in their work:

1. They must be fit for it
2. They must not do too much of it
3. They must have a sense of success in it

The Threefold Test of Mo Tzu

Mo Tzu (470–391 B.C.), the Chinese philosopher, applied three criteria to test all propositions:

1. Is it compatible with established conventions
2. Is it consistent with experience
3. Are the benefits desirable

Mo Tzu employed The Fourfold Standard to decide the last point.

The Fourfold Standard of Mo Tzu

The benefits Mo Tzu sought to encourage in the application of his Threefold Test were:

1. Enrichment of the poor
2. Increase in the population
3. Removal from danger
4. Regulation of disorder

Aristotle's Four Causes

These four causes, or types of relationships that produce an effect or result, are the:

1. Material Cause
2. Substantial Cause
3. Efficient Cause
4. Final Cause

The Four Degrees of Spiritual Evolution

According to Pythagoras, humans can be classified as part of four distinct stages:

1. Instinctive persons, the great majority, who are dominated by their will
2. Passionate persons, often artists or poets, in whom consciousness lives alongside will
3. Intellectual persons, often philosophers and leaders, who act chiefly out of intellectual activity
4. Initiates or adepts, those who have conquered self, who live selfless lives and help humanity evolve

The Five Agents

The Yin/Yang school of Chinese philosophy states that all cosmic forces are of two kinds: Yin, which is weak, passive, and negative; and Yang, which is strong, active, and positive. Interaction between the two creates all things. The Five Agents (*wu-hsing*) act with the Yin and Yang and are basic to life. The Five Agents are:

1. Metal
2. Wood
3. Water
4. Fire
5. Earth

Six Periods in the Cycle of Life

According to Pythagoras there are six phases in the cycle of existence:

1. Birth
2. Growth
3. Decay
4. Death
5. Absorption
6. Metamorphosis

Seven Types of Love

According to Plato there are seven types of love:

1. Love of man and woman
2. Love of parent and child
3. Love of a friend
4. Love of beauty
5. Love of good
6. Love of wisdom
7. Love of God

The Ten Categories

Aristotle named ten fundamental categories by which everything in the universe can be defined:

1. Being
2. Quantity
3. Quality
4. Relation
5. Doing

6. Suffering
7. Having (possessing)
8. Position
9. Place
10. Time

Arthur Schopenhauer

Schopenhauer's Thirty-eight Stratagems, or Thirty-eight Ways to Win an Argument

Arthur Schopenhauer (1788–1860), was a brilliant German philosopher. These thirty-eight Stratagems are excerpts from *The Art of Controversy*, first translated into English and published in 1896. Schopenhauer's thirty-eight ways to win an argument are:

1. Carry your opponent's proposition beyond its natural limits; exaggerate it. The more general your opponent's statement becomes, the more objections you can find against it. The more restricted and narrow your own propositions remain, the easier they are to defend. *Example:* Person #1 declares that the Peace of 1814 gave back independence to all the German towns of the Hanseatic League. Person # 2 gives an instance to the contrary by reciting the fact that Danzig, which received its independence from Napoleon, lost it by that Peace. Person #1 saves himself thus: "I said 'all German towns,' and Danzig was in Poland."

2. Use different meanings of your opponent's words to refute his or her argument. *Example:* Person A says, "You are not yet initiated into the mysteries of the Kantian philosophy." Person B replies, "Oh, if it's mysteries you're talking of, I'll have nothing to do with them.

3. Another trick is to ignore your opponent's proposition, which was intended to refer to a particular thing. Rather, understand it in some quite different sense, and then refute it. Attack something different than that which was asserted.

4. Hide your conclusion from your opponent till the end. Mingle your premises here and there in your talk. Get your opponent to agree to them in no definite order. By this circuitous route you conceal your game until you have obtained all the admissions that are necessary to reach your goal.

5. Use your opponent's beliefs against him. If the opponent refuses to accept your premises, use his own premises to your advantage. *Example:* If the opponent is a member of an organization or a religious sect to which you do not belong, you may employ the declared opinions of this group against the opponent.

6. Another plan is to confuse the issue by changing your opponent's words or what he or she seeks to prove. *Example:* Call something a different name: "good repute" instead of "honor," "virtue" instead of "virginity," "red-blooded" instead of "vertebrates."

7. State your proposition and show the truth of it by asking the opponent many questions. By asking many wide-reaching questions at once, you may hide what you want to get admitted. Then you quickly propound the argument resulting from the opponent's admissions.

8. Make your opponent angry. An angry person is less capable of using judgment or perceiving where his or her advantage lies.

9. Use your opponent's answers to your question to reach different or even opposite conclusions.

10. If your opponent answers all your questions negatively and refuses to grant you any points, ask him or her to concede the opposite of your premises. This may confuse the opponent as to which point you actually seek them to concede.

11. If the opponent grants you the truth of some of your premises, refrain from asking him or her to agree to your conclusion. Later, introduce your conclusion as a settled and admitted fact. Your opponent and others in attendance may come to believe that your conclusion was admitted.

12. If the argument turns upon general ideas with no particular names, you must use language or a metaphor that is favorable to your proposition. *Example:* What an impartial person would call "public worship" or a "system of religion," is described by an adherent as "piety" or "godliness," and by an opponent as "bigotry" or "superstition." In other words, insert what you intend to prove into the definition of the idea.

13. To make your opponent accept a proposition, you must give him or her an opposite, counter-proposition as well. If the contrast is glaring, the opponent will accept your proposition to avoid being paradoxical. *Eample:* If you want him to admit that a boy must do everything his father tells him to do, ask him "whether in all things we must obey or disobey our parents." Or, if a thing is said to occur "often," you are to understand few or many times, the opponent will say "many." It is as though you were to put gray next to black and call it white; or gray next to white and call it black.

14. Try to bluff your opponent. If he or she has answered several of your questions without the answers turning out in favor of your conclusion, advance your conclusion triumphantly, even if it does not follow. If your opponent is shy or stupid, and you yourself possess a great deal of impudence and a good voice, the trick may easily succeed.

15. If you wish to advance a proposition that is difficult to prove, put it aside for the moment. Instead, submit for your opponent's acceptance or rejection some true proposition, as though you wished to draw your proof from it. Should the opponent reject it because he or she suspects a trick, you can obtain your triumph by showing how absurd the opponent is to reject a true proposition. Should the opponent accept it, you now have reason on your side for the moment. You can either try to prove your original proposition, or as in #14, maintain that your original proposition is proved by what the opponent accepted. For this an extreme degree of impudence is required, but experience shows cases of it succeeding.

16. When your opponent puts forth a proposition, find it inconsistent with his or her other statements, beliefs, actions, or lack of action. *Example:* Should the opponent defend suicide, you may at once exclaim, "Why don't you hang yourself?" Should the opponent maintain that Berlin is an unpleasant place to live, you may say: "Why don't you leave on the first train?"

17. If your opponent presses you with a counter-proof, you will often be able to save yourself by advancing some subtle distinction. Try to find a second meaning or an ambiguous sense for your opponent's idea.

18. If your opponent has taken up a line of argument that will end in your defeat, you must not allow him or her to carry it to its conclusion. Interrupt the dispute, break it off altogether, or lead the opponent to a different subject.

19. Should your opponent expressly challenge you to produce any objection to some definite point in his or her argument, and you have nothing much to say, try to make the argument less specific. *Example:* If you are asked why a particular physical hypothesis cannot be accepted, you may speak of the fallibility of human knowledge, and give various illustrations of it.

20. If your opponent has admitted to all or most of your premises, do not ask him or her directly to accept your conclusion. Rather draw the conclusion yourself as if it too had been admitted.

21. When your opponent uses an argument that is superficial and you see the falsehood, you can, it is true, refute it by setting forth its superficial character. But it is better to meet the opponent with a counter-argument that is just as superficial, and so dispose of him or her. *For it is with victory that you are concerned, and not with truth. Example:* If the opponent appeals to prejudice, emotion, or attacks you personally, return the attack in the same manner.

22. If your opponent asks you to admit something from which the point in dispute will immediately follow, you must refuse to do so, declaring that it begs the question.

23. Contradiction and contention irritate a person into exaggerating their statements. By contradicting your opponent you may drive him or her into extending the statement beyond its natural limit. When you then contradict the exaggerated form of it, you look as though you had refuted the original statement. Contrarily, if

your opponent tries to extend your own statement further than you intended, redefine your statement's limits and say: "That is what I said, no more."

24. This trick consists in stating a false syllogism. Your opponent makes a proposition, and by false inference and distortion of his or her ideas you force from the proposition other propositions that are not intended and that appear absurd. It then appears the opponent's proposition gave rise to these inconsistencies, and so appears to be indirectly refuted.

25. If your opponent is making a generalization, find an instance to the contrary. Only one valid contradiction is needed to over-throw the opponent's proposition. *Example:* "All ruminants are horned" is a generalization that may be upset by the single in-stance of the camel.

26. A brilliant move is to turn the tables and use your opponent's arguments against him- or herself. *Example:* Your opponent de-clares, "So-and-so is a child, you must make an allowance for him." You retort, "Just *because* he is a child, I must correct him; otherwise he will persist in his bad habits."

27. Should your opponent surprise you by becoming particularly angry at an argument, you must urge it with all the more zeal. Not only will this make the opponent angry, it may be presumed that you have put your finger on the weak side of his or her case, and that the opponent is more open to attack on this point than you expected.

28. This trick is chiefly practicable in a dispute if there is an audience who is not an expert on the subject. You make an invalid objection to your opponent who seems to be defeated in the eyes of the audience. This strategy is particularly effective if your objection makes the opponent look ridiculous or if the audience laughs. If the opponent must make a long, complicated explanation to correct you, the audience will not be disposed to listen.

29. If you find that you are being beaten, you can create a diversion —that is, you can suddenly begin to talk of something else, as though it had a bearing on the matter in dispute. This may be done without presumption if the diversion has some general bearing on the matter.

30. Make an appeal to authority rather than reason. If your opponent respects an authority or an expert, quote that authority to further your case. If needed, quote what the authority said in some other sense or circumstance. Authorities that your opponent fails to understand are those which he or she generally admires the most.

     You may also, should it be necessary, not only twist your authorities, but actually falsify them, or quote something that you have invented entirely yourself.

31. If you know that you have no reply to the arguments that your opponent advances, you may by a fine stroke of irony, declare yourself to be an incompetent judge. *Example:* "What you say passes my poor powers of comprehension; it may well be all very true, but I can't understand it, and I refrain from any expression of opinion on it." In this way you insinuate to the bystanders,

with whom you are in good repute, that what your opponent says is nonsense. This is a trick that may be used only when you are quite sure that the audience thinks much better of you than your opponent.

32. A quick way of getting rid of an opponent's assertion, or of throwing suspicion on it, is by putting it into some odious category. *Example:* You can say, "That is Idealism," or "Atheism," or "Spiritualism," or "Mysticism." In making an objection of this kind you take for granted 1) That the assertion or question is identical with, or at least contained in, the category cited, and 2) The system referred to has been entirely refuted.

33. You admit your opponent's premises but deny the conclusion. *Example:* "That's all very well in theory, but it won't do in practice."

34. When you state a question or an argument, and your opponent gives you no direct answer, or evades it with a counter-question, or tries to change the subject, it is a sure sign you have touched a weak spot, sometimes without knowing it. You have, as it were, reduced the opponent to silence. You must, therefore, urge the point all the more, and not let your opponent evade it, even when you do not know where the weakness that you have hit upon really lies.

35. This trick makes all others unnecessary if it works. Instead of working on an opponent's intellect, work on his or her motive. If you succeed in making your opponent's opinion, should it prove

true, seem distinctly prejudicial to his or her own interest, the opponent will drop it like a hot potato. *Example:* A clergyman is defending some philosophical dogma. You make him sensible of the fact that it is in immediate contradiction with a fundamental doctrine of his church. He will abandon his argument.

36. You may also puzzle and bewilder your opponent by mere bombast. If the opponent is weak or does not wish to appear as if he or she has no idea what you are talking about, you can easily impose upon him some argument that sounds very deep or learned, or that sounds indisputable.

37. Should your opponent be in the right but, luckily for you, choose a faulty proof, you can easily refute it and then claim that you have refuted the whole position. This is the way in which bad advocates lose a good case. If no accurate proof occurs to the opponent or the bystanders, you have won the day.

38. A last trick is to become personal, insulting, and rude as soon as you perceive that your opponent has the upper hand. In becoming personal you leave the subject altogether, and turn your attack on the person by remarks of an offensive and spiteful character. This is a very popular trick, because everyone is able to carry it into effect.

PLANTS AND ANIMALS

The Six Categories of Dogs

Today there are more than 100 breeds of dogs. They can be classified in six groups:

1. Working dogs, including collies, mastiffs, schnauzers, sheepdogs, and the Siberian husky

The collie, a working dog

2. Sporting dogs, including pointers, setters, and retrievers

The pointer, a sporting dog

3. Hounds, including bassets, bloodhounds, dachshunds, foxhounds, and greyhounds

The basset hound

4. Terriers, including fox, Welsh, Scottish terriers, and airedales

The fox terrier

5. Nonsporting dogs, including chow chows, poodles, dalmatians, and bulldogs

The chow chow, a nonsporting dog

6. Toy dogs, including pekingese and chihuahuas

The pekingese, a toy dog

The Seven Types of Cats

All felines can be loosely organized into these categories:

1. Great cats, including lions, tigers, leopards, snow leopards, and jaguars
2. Lesser cats, including ocelots, leopard cats, tabby cats, desert cats, plain cats, and marbled cats
3. Other cats, including pumas, clouded leopards, and golden cats
4. Lynxes, including jungle cats, caracals, northern lynxes, and bobcats
5. Servals
6. Jaguarondis
7. Cheetahs

The Twelve Major Types of Fruit

Although some of the examples below are considered vegetables by most people, botanists consider all these to be fruits:

1. Berries, a fleshy fruit that usually has many seeds embedded throughout, such as tomatoes, grapes, and currants
2. Hesperidium, which resemble the berry but has a leathery rind and sacs filled with juice, such as oranges, lemons, and grapefruits
3. Pepos, which have a hard outer covering, such as cucumbers, squash, and pumpkins
4. Drupes, a fleshy fruit with a thin outer skin and a pit or stone at the center, such as cherries, plums, and peaches
5. Aggregates, which consist of a cluster of small fruitlets, such as blackberries, raspberries, and strawberries
6. Multiple fruits, which are formed from the individual ovaries of multiple flowers, such as the pineapple, fig, and mulberry
7. Pomes, a fleshy fruit with a thin skin and seed-containing compartments at the center, such as apples and pears
8. Legumes, which have seeds encased in a single pod, such as peas and lima beans
9. Capsules, similar to a legume but has more than one compartment with seeds, such as okras
10. Caryposis, which has a tough outer layer that is firmly attached to the seed coat, such as a kernel of sweet corn
11. Nuts, a hard, dry fruit with a single seed usually enclosed in a husk, such as chestnuts and filberts (but not peanuts, which are technically legumes)
12. Dry fruits, including the relatively unknown fruits of grains, flowers, and other plants

The Nineteen Orders of Mammals

There are over 5,000 species of mammals, ranging from the shrew, which is 2 inches long, to the whale, which can be 100 feet long. All mammals can be classified in these nineteen orders:

Order	*Examples*
1. Artiodactyla (even-toed, hoofed mammals)	antelopes, cattle, deer, pigs
2. Carnivora (flesh-eating mammals)	cats, dogs, bears, raccoons
3. Cetacea	whales, dolphins
4. Chiroptera (flying mammals)	bats
5. Dermoptera (gliding mammals)	flying lemur
6. Edentata	anteaters, sloths, armadillos
7. Hyracoidea	hyraxes
8. Insectivora (insect-eating mammals)	moles and shrews
9. Logomorpha	rabbits and hares
10. Marsupialia (pouched mammals)	opossums, koalas, kangaroos
11. Monotremata (egg-laying mammals)	duckbills
12. Perissodactyla (odd-toed, hoofed mammals)	horses, zebras, rhinoceroses

13. Pholidota   pangolins
    (scaly mammals)
14. Pinnipedia   seals, sea lions
    (fin-footed mammals)
15. Primates   lemurs, monkeys, baboons
16. Proboscidea   elephant
17. Rodentia   beavers, squirrels, mice
    (gnawing mammals)
18. Sirenia   manatees, sea cows
19. Tubulidentata   aardvark

The Twenty-eight Orders of Birds

There are slightly less than 9,000 species of birds, Birds are of the phylum *Chordata*, subphylum *Vertebrata*, and class *Aves*. They are organized into twenty-eight orders:

Order

Examples

1. Anseriformes   duck, goose, swan
2. Apodiformes   swift, hummingbird
3. Apteryciformes   kiwi
4. Caprimulgiformes   nightjar, nighthawk, potoo
5. Casuariiformes   cassowaries, emo
6. Charadriiformes   gull, puffin, tern
7. Ciconiiformes   bittern, heron, ibis, stork
8. Coliiformes   mousebird
9. Columbiformes   pigeon, dove

10. Coraciiformes	bee eater, hornbill, kingfisher
11. Cuculiformes	cuckoo, turaco
12. Falconiformes	condor, eagle, falcon, hawk
13. Galliformes	grouse, partridge, turkey
14. Gaviiformes	loon
15. Gruiformes	rail, coot, crane
16. Passeriformes	bluebird, canary, crow, swallow

Mocking bird

17. Pelecaniformes	pelican, cormorant
18. Phoenicopteriformes	flamingo
19. Piciformes	woodpecker, toucan
20. Podicepediformes	grebe
21. Procellariiformes	petrel, albatross
22. Psittaciformes	cockatoo, lovebird, macaw, parrot
23. Rheiformes	rhea
24. Sphenisciformes	penguin
25. Strigiformes	owls
26. Struthioniformes	ostrich
27. Tinamiformes	tinamous
28. Trogoniformes	trogon

POLITICS

The first Democratic donkey appeared in this Thomas Nast cartoon in 1870.

The first Republican elephant was seen in a Thomas Nast cartoon four years later.

The Gang of Four   In China during the Cultural Revolution of the 1960s and 1970s, four low-ranking officials gained the favor of Mao Tse-tung and advanced to high positions in the government. With Mao's death in 1976 the Gang of Four lost power and were imprisoned. The members were:

1. Chaing Ch'ing, Mao's second wife
2. Wang Hung-wen
3. Chang Ch'un-ch'iou
4. Yao Wen-yuan

The Fort Dix Five   In June 1969, military prisoners rioted at the stockade at Fort Dix, New Jersey. Five of these prisoners were brought before the court martial for arson and conspiracy to riot. They were:

1. William Brakefield
2. Thomas Catlow
3. Carlos Rodrigues-Torres
4. Jeffrey Russell
5. Terry Klug (the only one acquitted)

The Vancouver Five   In 1982 five young political activists were convicted for a series of bombings in Canada, which included destruction of a factory, power plant, and warehouse. The Vancouver Five were:

1. Julie Belmas
2. Gerry Hannah
3. Ann Hansen
4. Doug Stewart
5. Brent Taylor

The Harrisburg Six

In January 1971, six political activists were accused of plotting to sabotage federal buildings in Washington and planning to kidnap Henry Kissinger. Called the Harrisburg Six, they were:

1. Eqbal Ahmed
2. Philip F. Berrigan
3. Elizabeth McAlister
4. Neil McLaughlin
5. Anthony Scoblick
6. Joseph Wenderoth

The Watergate Seven

In 1972, seven men broke into, "bugged," and performed other acts of political espionage at the Democratic National Committee headquarters in the Watergate building, Washington, D.C. These seven men, later convicted, were:

1. Bernard L. Baker
2. Virgilio R. Gonzalez
3. E. Howard Hunt, Jr.
4. G. Gordon Liddy
5. James W. McCord
6. Eugenio Martinez
7. Frank A. Sturgis

The Chicago Seven

From activities and disturbances relating to the Democratic National Convention in Chicago in 1968, seven men were convicted in 1970 of conspiracy to incite a riot, contempt of court, and other charges. An eighth defendant, Bobby Seale, was tried separately. The Chicago Seven were:

1. Rennie Davis
2. David T. Dellinger
3. John Froines
4. Thomas Hayden
5. Abbie Hoffman
6. Jerry C. Rubin
7. Lee Weiner

The Chicago Seven and Bobby Seale. From left to right: (top row) Jerry Rubin, Abbie Hoffman, Tom Hayden, Rennie Davis, (bottom row) Bobby Seale, Lee Weiner, John Froines and David Dellinger

The New York Eight

In 1984 in Brooklyn, N.Y., eight political activists were charged with racketeering, conspiracy to rob armored cars, weapons possession, and other crimes. They were convicted on the charges of weapons possession and the use of false identity. They were:

1. Howard Bonds (later a government witness)
2. Ruth Carter
3. Coltrain Chimurenga
4. Omowale Clay
5. Yvette Kelly
6. Viola Plummer
7. Roger Taylor
8. Roger Wareham

The Catonsville Nine

In May 1967, nine Vietnam war protestors were charged with destroying government property and interfering with the military draft in Catonsville, Maryland. The protestors were:

1. Daniel Berrigan
2. Philip F. Berrigan
3. David Durst
4. John Hogan
5. Thomas P. Lewis
6. Marjorie B. Melville
7. Thomas Melville
8. George Mische
9. Mary Moylan

The Hollywood Ten

When called before the House Committee on Un-American Activities in 1947, ten Hollywood figures refused to testify. These people were eventually imprisoned for contempt:

1. Alvah Bessie
2. Herbert Biberman
3. Lester Cole
4. Edward Dmytryk
5. Ring Lardner, Jr.
6. John Howard Lawson
7. Albert Maltz
8. Samuel Ornitz
9. Adrian Scott
10. Dalton Trumbo

The Wilmington Ten

Nine black men and one white woman were initially convicted and imprisoned after racial rioting in Wilmington, North Carolina, in 1972. Their convictions were overturned by an appeals court in 1980, after prosecution witnesses withdrew their testimony. The ten defendants were:

1. Benjamin Chavis
2. Reginald Epps
3. Jerry Jacobs
4. James McKoy
5. Wayne Moor
6. Marvin Patrick
7. Connie Tindall
8. Anne Shephard Turner
9. Willi Earl Vereen
10. Joe Wright

The Wells Fargo Thirteen

In 1985, fourteen people were accused of robbing a Wells Fargo armored car of over $7 million in Hartford, Connecticut, to finance Puerto Rican independence. One, Ann Gassin, turned government witness. The remaining defendants became known as the Wells Fargo Thirteen:

1. Carlos Ayes Suarez
2. Luz Maria Berrios
3. Isaac Camacho Negron
4. Elias Castro Ramos
5. Luis Alfredo Colon Osorio
6. Angel Diaz Ruiz
7. Jorge Farinacci Garcia
8. Hilton Fernandez Diamante
9. Orlando Gonzalez Claudio
10. Ivon Melendez Carrion
11. Filiberto Ojeda Rios
12. Norman Ramirez Talavera
13. Juan Enrique Segarra Palmer

PSYCHOLOGY

Sigmund Freud

The Three Stages of Childhood

According to Sigmund Freud, young children pass through three stages as the libido, or sexual part of their being, is formed. The stages are:

1. *Oral stage*, in which the baby's sexual sensation is limited to that of the lips and mouth while feeding
2. *Anal-Sadistic stage*, which occurs between ages two and four, when the child's libido is developed through its fascination with feces and the anus
3. *Phallic stage*, in which the child discovers the penis, or, in girls, the clitoris, as the focus of sexual sensation

The Three Parts of the Psyche

Freud divides our psychological being into these parts:

1. *The ego*, the essential core of a person that experiences and interacts with the outside world and acts as a balance between the id and the superego
2. *The id*, the primitive, animalistic part of our psyche
3. *The superego*, the conscience, which provokes guilt in us and governs our standards of conduct

The Four Types of Mental Illness

Although there are a large number of emotional and mental illnesses, the most common ones can be classified into these categories:

1. Depression and manic depression
2. Schizophrenia, with symptoms including hallucination, delusions, and disordered thinking
3. Anxiety disorders, including phobias, panic disorders, and obsessive-compulsive disorders
4. Eating disorders, such as anorexia nervosa and bulimia

The Five P's

This test, published by Variety Pre-Schooler's Workshop, assesses the behavioral, emotional, or developmental disorders in children from six to sixty months old. The titles stand for *Parent Professional Pre-school Performance Profile*. The five areas it measures are:

1. Routines and self-help skills
2. Motor development
3. Language
4. Social development
5. Cognitive skills

Eight-State Questionnaire

This test, published by the Institute for Personality and Ability Testing, Inc., is used in counseling adolescents and adults by evaluating their state of mind. The eight key mood states it measures are:

1. Anxiety
2. Stress
3. Depression
4. Regression
5. Fatigue
6. Guilt
7. Extraversion
8. Arousal

SCIENCE AND NATURE

San Francisco after the earthquake of 1906

The Three Dimensions

Our perception of space is defined by three dimensions, or planes:

1. Height (the vertical plane)
2. Width (the horizontal plane)
3. Depth (the sagittal plane)

We perceive one-dimensional space as a dot. When the first two planes intersect we perceive a flat line. When the third plane is added we perceive three-dimensional space. Scientists theorize that a fourth dimension—time—also exists.

The Three States of Matter

Matter can exist in these three states:

1. Solid
2. Liquid

3. Gas

The Three Primary Colors

When properly mixed, these three primary colors will produce all the colors of the spectrum:

1. Red
2. Green

3. Blue

Newton's Three Laws of Motion

In the seventeenth century Isaac Newton first developed these three laws concerning the movement of objects:

1. An object will remain motionless or will move in a straight line unless acted on by a force.
2. The acceleration of an object is directly proportional to force acting upon it, and inversely proportional to the object's mass.
3. For every action, there is an equal and opposite reaction.

———

The Three Laws of Thermodynamics

These three laws concerning heat are true of all matter in the universe:

1. Energy tends to be conserved: in a system where no outside forces act upon it, the energy will remain constant.
2. Unless some outside force acts upon it, heat will not flow from a cold object to a hot one.
3. Given a finite number of attempts it is impossible to reduce a substance to a temperature of absolute zero (a hypothetical point at 273 degrees on the Celsius scale).

———

The Three-Age System

In 1836 a Danish museum director created the system used by archaeologists to date ancient tools and implements. Although the system does not apply in the Americas, Australia, or on many Pacific islands, it can be used throughout the rest of the world. The Three Ages are:

1. The Stone Age

2. The Bronze Age
3. The Iron Age

The Four
Eras and Twelve Periods
of Geologic Time

ERA	APPROX. AGE IN MILLIONS OF YEARS (Radioactivity)	PERIOD (System) Period refers to a time measure; system refers to the rocks deposited during a period.		
CENOZOIC	2 7 25 37 54 65	Quaternary { Recent / Pleistocene } Man · Neogene Tertiary { Pliocene / Miocene / Oligocene / Eocene / Paleocene } Paleogene · Mammals		
MESOZOIC	135 190 220–230	Cretaceous Jurassic — Flying reptiles / First bird Triassic — Dinosaurs		
PALEOZOIC	280 345 400 435 500 570–600	Permian Pennsylvanian } Carboniferous — First reptiles Mississippian Devonian — First amphibian — First insect fossils Silurian — First land plant fossils Ordovician — First vertebrate fossil (fish) Cambrian		
PRECAMBRIAN	700 3400 4000 4500	First multicellular organisms First one-celled organisms Approximate age of oldest rocks discovered Approximate age of meteorites		

The Five Layers of the Earth's Atmosphere

The layers of our atmosphere are characterized by the ranges of temperatures they contain and their distance from the surface. The layers are:

1. The troposphere, the lowest layer, which extends to a height of 5 to 6 miles at the poles and 10 to 11 miles in the tropics. All weather that we experience occurs in this layer.
2. The stratosphere, which extends 30 miles above the earth
3. The mesosphere, which extends 50 miles
4. The thermosphere, which extends 300 miles
5. The exosphere, which extends beyond the 300 miles where the earth's atmosphere merges with the gases of space.

The Six Layers of the Earth

Although geologists cannot see the earth's interior, they believe these six layers exist:

Layer	*Range of Depth*
1. Crust	6–40 miles (from the surface)
2. Upper mantle	40–600 miles
3. Lower mantle	600–1,700 miles
4. Outer core	1,700–2,800 miles
5. Transition region	2,800–3,090 miles
6. Inner core	3,090–5,022 miles

The Seven Colors of the Spectrum

Known to every student as ROY G. BIV, the colors are:

1. Red
2. Orange
3. Yellow
4. Green

5. Blue
6. Indigo
7. Violet

The Nine Magnitudes of the Richter Earthquake Scale

This scale of earthquake magnitude, devised by Seismologist Charles F. Richter in 1935, measures the energy released at a quake's center. The scale is logarithmic, which means a quake measuring four on the Richter scale has *ten* times the released energy as a quake measuring three. Here are the correlations between magnitudes and the expected intensity:

Magnitude	*Likely Effects*
1	detectable by instruments only
2	difficult to perceive
3	may be felt
4.5	Detectable by people within 20 miles of epicenter; slight damage possible

Magnitude	*Likely Effects*
6	moderately destructive
7	a major earthquake
8	a great earthquake
9	theoretically possible but has never occurred during human history

The famous San Francisco earthquake of 1906 measured 7.8 on the Richter scale. The Alaska quake in 1964 measured 8.4.

The Nine Major Types of Coal

Coal was formed from the remains of plants in earlier geological periods. It accounts for over 55 percent of the electrical power produced in the United States today. The nine major types of coal are:

1. Anthracite
2. Semianthracite
3. Semibituminous
4. Bituminous
5. Subbituminous
6. Lignite
7. Peat
8. Peat coal
9. Cannel

The Ten Cloud Genera

This scheme classifies the major types of clouds into these ten categories:

High Altitude

1. Cirrus is composed of ice crystals and appears as thin, white streaks or tufts without shadows.
2. Cirrocumulus looks like white ripples and billows arranged in lines. It is sometimes called "mackerel sky."
3. Cirrostratus looks like a thin whitish veil that can cover the entire sky. It often produces halo effects around the sun or moon.

Middle Altitude

4. Altocumulus appears as flattened globular masses or rolls that are shaded from white to black. These water clouds are *also* called "mackerel sky."
5. Altostratus looks like a translucent or opaque bluish or gray sheet through which the moon and sun can sometimes be seen. This cloud does precipitate.
6. Nimbostratus is a large gray or dark cloud that produces continuous rain or snow.

Low Altitude

7. Stratocumulus contains lines or rolls of white and dark clouds grouped closely together.

8. Stratus is a uniform gray cloud that often develops from fog and rises above the ground.

9. Cumulus is a fair-weather cloud that has a flat base and high white domes or tufts. It is a brilliant white when illuminated by the sun, although it does occasionally produce showers.

A cumulus cloud drawn by Leonardo da Vinci

Various Altitudes

10. Cumulonimbus is a thunderstorm cloud that can occur at all altitudes, is very dense, and often appears as a towering wall with striking contrasts of light and dark.

The Fifteen Tectonic Plates

Geologists who study the earth's surface believe these are the main plates that can move independently of each other:

1. African Plate
2. Antarctic Plate
3. Arabian Plate
4. Caribbean Plate
5. Caroline Plate
6. Cocos Plate
7. Eurasian Plate
8. Indian-Australian Plate
9. Juan De Fuca Plate
10. Nazca Plate
11. North American Plate
12. Pacific Plate
13. Philippine Plate
14. Scotia Plate
15. South American Plate

The 103 Elements of the Periodic Table

A total of 103 elements have been discovered so far. The newest discoveries are found only in unstable form and exist for very short amounts of time. The elements are:

Atomic Number	Element	Symbol
1	Hydrogen	H
2	Helium	He
3	Lithium	Li
4	Beryllium	Be
5	Boron	B
6	Carbon	C

Atomic Number	Element	Symbol
7	Nitrogen	N
8	Oxygen	O
9	Fluorine	F
10	Neon	Ne
11	Sodium	Na
12	Magnesium	Mg
13	Aluminum	Al
14	Silicon	Si
15	Phosphorus	P
16	Sulphur	S
17	Chlorine	Cl
18	Argon	Ar
19	Potassium	K
20	Calcium	Ca
21	Scandium	Sc
22	Titanium	Ti
23	Vanadium	V
24	Chromium	Cr
25	Manganese	Mn
26	Iron	Fe
27	Cobalt	Co
28	Nickel	Ni
29	Copper	Cu
30	Zinc	Zn
31	Gallium	Ga
32	Germanium	Ge

Atomic Number	Element	Symbol
33	Arsenic	As
34	Selenium	Se
35	Bromine	Br
36	Krypton	Kr
37	Rubidium	Rb
38	Strontium	Sr
39	Yttrium	Y
40	Zirconium	Zr
41	Niobium	Nb
42	Molybdenum	Mo
43	Technetium	Tc
44	Ruthenium	Ru
45	Rhodium	Rh
46	Palladium	Pd
47	Silver	Ag
48	Cadmium	Cd
49	Indium	In
50	Tin	Sn
51	Antimony	Sb
52	Tellurium	Te
53	Iodine	I
54	Xenon	Xe
55	Cesium	Cs
56	Barium	Ba
57	Lanthanum	La
58	Cerium	Ce

Atomic Number	*Element*	*Symbol*
59	Praseodymium	Pr
60	Neodymium	Nd
61	Promethium	Pm
62	Samarium	Sm
63	Europium	Eu
64	Gadolinium	Gd
65	Terbium	Tb
66	Dysprosium	Dy
67	Holmium	Ho
68	Erbium	Er
69	Thulium	Tm
70	Ytterbium	Yb
71	Lutetium	Lu
72	Hafnium	Hf
73	Tantalum	Ta
74	Tungsten	W
75	Rhenium	Re
76	Osmium	Os
77	Iridium	Ir
78	Platinum	Pt
79	Gold	Au
80	Mercury	Hg
81	Thallium	Ti
82	Lead	Pb
83	Bismuth	Bi
84	Polonium	Po

Atomic Number	Element	Symbol
85	Astatine	At
86	Radon	Rn
87	Francium	Fr
88	Radium	Ra
89	Actinium	Ac
90	Thorium	Th
91	Protactinium	Pa
92	Uranium	U

The element, uranium

93	Neptunium	Np
94	Plutonium	Pu
95	Americium	Am
96	Curium	Cm
97	Berkelium	Bk
98	Californium	Cf
99	Einsteinium	Es
100	Fermium	Fm
101	Mendelevium	Md
102	Nobelium	No
103	Lawrencium	Lr

SPORTS AND GAMES

Secretariat

The Big Three

In collegiate sports, the Big Three are three members of the Ivy League:

1. Harvard
2. Princeton
3. Yale

The Triple Crown

The three most famous horse races in the United States make up the Triple Crown. They are:

1. The Kentucky Derby
2. The Preakness
3. The Belmont Stakes

Only eleven horses have won the Crown by winning all three races in the same year:

Year	Horse	Year	Horse
1919	Sir Barton	1946	Assault
1930	Gallant Fox	1948	Citation
1935	Omaha	1973	Secretariat
1937	War Admiral	1977	Seattle Slew
1941	Whirlaway	1978	Affirmed
1943	Count Fleet		

The Triathlon From the Greek for three—*tri*—and for contest—*athlon*—comes the Triathlon. This modern athletic competition consists of a:

1. 2.4-mile swim
2. followed immediately by a 112-mile bike race
3. ending with a 26.2-mile marathon run

————

The Fearsome Foursome In the 1960s, the Fearsome Foursome was the nickname given to four members of the Los Angeles Rams' defensive line. They were:

1. Roosevelt (Rosie) Greer
2. Deacon Jones
3. Lamar Lundy
4. Merlin Olsen

————

The Four Horsemen The Four Horsemen, not of the Apocalypse, but of Notre Dame's football team of 1924, were members of its legendary backfield. Named the Four Horsemen by Grantland Rice of the *New York Herald Tribune*, the four team members were:

1. Jim Crowley
2. Elmer Layden
3. Don Miller
4. Harry Stuldreher

The *Four Horsemen,* University of Notre Dame, 1924

The Pentathlon

The Pentathlon is a series of five track-and-field events in which the athletes' overall scores were based on their scores in the individual events. For women, the five events are the:

1. 800 meter
2. 100-meter hurdles
3. high jump
4. long jump
5. shot put

For men, the events are the:

1. 200 meter
2. 1,500 meter
3. discus throw
4. javelin throw
5. long jump

For the modern Olympic Pentathlon, the events are:

1. cross-country running
2. fencing
3. horseback riding
4. pistol shooting
5. swimming

The Six Categories in Trivial Pursuit

In this popular board game, which tests your knowledge of trivia, there are six categories of questions:

1. Geography (blue spaces on the board)
2. Entertainment (pink spaces)

3. History (yellow spaces)
4. Art & Literature (brown spaces)
5. Science & Nature (green spaces)
6. Sports & Leisure (orange spaces)

The Heptathlon

The Heptathlon is a track-and-field contest that has seven individual events. The competitor's overall score is derived from the individual scores. The events are the:

1. 100 meter
2. 800 meter
3. 100-meter hurdles
4. high jump
5. javelin throw
6. long jump
7. shot put

The Seven Blocks of Granite

The Seven Blocks of Granite were members of the 1936 Fordham University football team. These players were;

1. Al Babartshy
2. Johnny Druze
3. Ed Franco
4. Vince Lombardi
5. Leo Paquin
6. Nat Pierce
7. Alex Wojciechowicz

The Big Eight

The Big Eight names the college athletic conference of which the following schools are members:

1. University of Colorado
2. Iowa State University
3. University of Kansas
4. Kansas State University
5. University of Missouri
6. University of Nebraska
7. University of Oklahoma
8. Oklahoma State University

The Eight Parries

In the art of fencing, there are eight positions for parry or thrust of the foil:

1. Prime
2. Seconde
3. Tierce
4. Quarte
5. Quinte
6. Sixte
7. Septime
8. Octave

The Nine Hands in Poker

Assuming no wild cards are used, these nine hands are possible ranked from strongest to weakest:

1. Straight flush—five cards in the same suit and in sequence
2. Four-of-a-kind—any four cards of the same rank
3. Full house—three-of-a-kind and one pair
4. Flush—five cards of the same suit, not all in sequence
5. Straight—five cards in sequence, but not all the same suit
6. Three-of-a-kind—three cards of the same rank
7. Two pair—two cards of the same rank and others of a different rank
8. One pair—two cards of the same rank
9. High card—five unmatched and unrelated cards

The Big Ten

The teams of the following academic institutions make up the athletic conference known as The Big Ten:

1. University of Illinois
2. Indiana University
3. University of Iowa
4. University of Michigan
5. Michigan State University
6. University of Minnesota
7. Northwestern University
8. Ohio State University
9. Purdue University
10. University of Wisconsin

The Decathlon

This Olympic competition for men, the Decathlon, consists of ten track-and-field events. The events are scored individually, and then combined to determine the competitor's overall score. The ten events are the:

1. 100 meter
2. 400 meter
3. 1,500 meter
4. 110-meter hurdles
5. high jump
6. long jump
7. javelin throw
8. pole vault
9. shot put
10. discus throw

The Pacific Ten

This college athletic conference is composed of ten competing institutions, clustered primarily along the West Coast. The ten schools are:

Ten

1. University of Arizona
2. Arizona State University

3. University of California at Berkeley
4. University of California at Los Angeles
5. University of Oregon
6. Oregon State University
7. University of Southern California
8. Stanford University
9. University of Washington
10. Washington State University

———

The Forty Spaces on the MONOPOLY® Game Board

Since 1935 the board of this Parker Brothers game has had these forty spaces on which players can land:

1. Collect $200.00 Salary as You Pass Go
2. Mediterranean Avenue, Price $60
3. Community Chest
4. Baltic Avenue, Price $60
5. Income Tax. Pay 10% or $200
6. Reading Railroad, Price $200
7. Oriental Avenue, Price $100
8. Chance
9. Vermont Avenue, Price $100
10. Connecticut Avenue, Price $120
11. In Jail, or Just Visiting
12. St. Charles Place, Price $140
13. Electric Company, Price $140
14. States Avenue, Price $140
15. Virginia Avenue, Price $160

16. Pennsylvania Railroad, Price $200
17. St. James Place, Price $180
18. Community Chest
19. Tennessee Avenue, Price $180
20. New York Avenue, Price $200
21. Free Parking
22. Kentucky Avenue, Price $220
23. Chance
24. Indiana Avenue, Price $220
25. Illinois Avenue, Price $240
26. B & O Railroad, Price $200
27. Atlantic Avenue, Price $260
28. Ventnor Avenue, Price $260
29. Water Works, Price $150
30. Marvin Gardens, Price $280
31. Go to Jail
32. Pacific Avenue, Price $300
33. North Carolina Avenue, Price $300
34. Community Chest
35. Pennsylvania Avenue, Price $320
36. Short Line, Price $200
37. Chance
38. Park Place, Price $350
39. Luxury Tax. Pay $75
40. Boardwalk, Price $400

Index